God's Unbreakable Oath

Volume 1

God's Unbreakable Oath

Tracing the Ways God Redeems His Whole Creation

Volume 1
Sacrifice

Colin Cook

WIPF & STOCK · Eugene, Oregon

GOD'S UNBREAKABLE OATH, VOLUME 1
Tracing the Ways God Redeems His Whole Creation: Sacrifice

Copyright © 2025 Colin Cook. All rights reserved. Except for brief quotations in critical publications or reviews, no part of this book may be reproduced in any manner without prior written permission from the publisher. Write: Permissions, Wipf and Stock Publishers, 199 W. 8th Ave., Suite 3, Eugene, OR 97401.

Wipf & Stock
An Imprint of Wipf and Stock Publishers
199 W. 8th Ave., Suite 3
Eugene, OR 97401

www.wipfandstock.com

PAPERBACK ISBN: 979-8-3852-6425-4
HARDCOVER ISBN: 979-8-3852-6426-1
EBOOK ISBN: 979-8-3852-6427-8

VERSION NUMBER 12/23/25

All Scripture quotations, unless otherwise indicated, are taken from the New King James Version®. Copyright © 1982 by Thomas Nelson. Used by permission. All rights reserved.

Scripture quotations marked (BSB) are taken from The Holy Bible, Berean Standard Bible, BSB, produced in cooperation with Bible Hub, Discovery Bible, OpenBible.com, and the Berean Bible Translation Committee. This text of God's Word has been dedicated to the public domain.

Scripture quotations marked (CSB) are taken from the Christian Standard Bible®, Copyright © 2017 by Holman Bible Publishers. Used by permission. Christian Standard Bible® and CSB® are federally registered trademarks of Holman Bible Publishers.

Scripture quotations marked (ESV) are taken from the ESV® Bible (The Holy Bible, English Standard Version®), © 2001 by Crossway, a publishing ministry of Good News Publishers. ESV Text Edition: 2025. Used by permission. All rights reserved.

Scripture quotations marked (ISV) are taken from the Holy Bible: International

Standard Version® Release 2.0. Copyright © 1996–2013 by the ISV Foundation. Used by permission of Davidson Press, LLC. All rights reserved internationally.

Scripture quotations marked (KJV) are taken from the King James Version, public domain.

Scripture quotations marked (MSG) are taken from The Message, copyright © 1993, 2002, 2018 by Eugene H. Peterson. Used by permission of NavPress. All rights reserved. Represented by Tyndale House Publishers.

Scripture quotations marked (NASB) are taken from the (NASB®) New American Standard Bible®, Copyright © 1960, 1971, 1977, 1995, 2020 by The Lockman Foundation. Used by permission. All rights reserved. lockman.org

Scripture quotations marked (NEB) are taken from the New English Bible, copyright © Cambridge University Press and Oxford University Press 1961, 1970. All rights reserved.

Scripture quotations marked (NIV) are taken from The Holy Bible, International Version®, NIV®. Copyright © 1973, 1978, 1984, 2011 by Biblica, Inc. Used with permission of Zondervan. All rights reserved worldwide. www.zondervan.com

Scripture quotations marked (NLT) are taken from the Holy Bible, New Living Translation, copyright © 1996, 2004, 2015 by Tyndale House Foundation. Used by permission of Tyndale House Publishers, Inc., Carol Stream, Illinois 60188. All rights reserved.

Scripture quotations marked (REV) are taken from the Revised English Version® (REV®) Copyright © 2025 by Spirit & Truth Fellowship International. All rights reserved. RevisedEnglishVersion.com.

Scripture quotations marked (TLB) are taken from The Living Bible, copyright © 1971 by Tyndale House Foundation. Used by permission of Tyndale House Publishers, Carol Stream, Illinois 60188. All rights reserved.

Scripture quotations marked (WEY) are taken from the Weymouth New Testament by Richard Francis Weymouth, 1912. Public domain in the United States.

Italics in Scripture quotations are for emphasis and have been supplied by the author.

To my beloved sons, Chris and Bren,
and
Gan,
Rotimi, Ayomide,
Amit,
and
Nonso

O God, You have taught me from my youth;
And to this day I declare Your wondrous works.
Now also when I am old and grayheaded,
O God, do not forsake me,
Until I declare Your strength to this generation,
Your power to everyone who is to come.

Psalm 71:17–18

Contents

Preface | xi
Acknowledgments | xiii
Abbreviations | xv

Introduction   The Witness of Isaiah: God's Unbreakable Oath to All Humanity | 1

Chapter 1   The Witness of Ephesians/Colossians: God's Secret Plan | 12

Chapter 2   The Witness of the Gospel (1): God in Christ Carries the Judgment of the World | 21

Chapter 3   The Witness of the Gospel (2): Christ's Redemption Equal in Extent to Adam's Fall | 37

Chapter 4   The Witness of Faith (1): Faith—A Human Thing? Or a God Thing? | 63

Chapter 5   The Witness of Faith (2): How God Brings Faith to All Humanity | 77

Chapter 6   The Witness of Ezekiel (1): Israel's *Unfaithfulness* Testifies to the Salvation of All | 95

Chapter 7   The Witness of Ezekiel (2): The Saving of All Israel Mirrors the Saving of All Humanity | 120

A Preview of Volume 2 | 149

Index | 151

Preface

To believe in God's plan to save the whole human race requires a serious reexamination of the gospel. Plumbing its depths reveals a lot we have missed or that has remained undiscovered.

It's not enough to explore the texts that promise God's rescue of all—though we shall certainly do that. But such an exploration must be carried out with gospel context. For it is the gospel that *clarifies* the meaning of the promises, and that *guarantees* their fulfillment.

Without the gospel, the texts asserting God's salvation of all mankind fail to penetrate the modern Christian mind. They remain within the intellectual realm as "hope" or "possibility"—or downright heresy. But couched within the gospel they take on *force*. The gospel is a force—the compelling fact of God's sacrifice of his Son for a lost humanity. It is irresistible love for the human race that captures the heart. In that sacrifice is a mercy so infinite, so all-powerful that it swamps all opposition to it—even God's own judgments—until mercy, like a Lamb as one slain, reigning on the throne of final judgment, draws all creation to it in awe (Rev 5:13).

So in this book, *God's Unbreakable Oath*, we consider, in volume 1, the oath that will never be withdrawn which God made through the prophet Isaiah to reconcile all humanity to himself. The oath appears to be contradicted by the book of Revelation (see the Introduction). There, in the final judgment, the lost are described as being consigned to the lake of fire. So we examine the sacrifice of Christ for the sin of world. Does it reach those in the lake of fire? (See chs. 2 and 3.)

We then turn to the issue of faith, because for all the world to be saved means that all the world will come to trust in Christ. This book will show that faith comes as a gift along with the gospel itself. It does not flow from

Preface

the human will which is in bondage. By grace we believe. God is able to, and will, position each person to receive faith (see chs. 4 and 5). Next, the issue of *how* God does that—bring all people to belief—is investigated.

Faith in Christ is unique. It is a response to crisis. Through God's sovereignty, God is able to bring each person to the end of their resources, either here or in the final judgment. Faith, almost violent in its approach, breaks into the soul that has been numbed by the assaults of the world. It is by grace we believe in the seemingly impossible (see ch. 5). And God has his ways of opening us up—both here and in the final judgment—to receiving faith. Which leads to an inquiry into God's judgments because judgments are God's response to willful unbelief.

We examine the prophet Ezekiel's message. He affirms that judgments lead not to *final* destruction but to humanity coming to know that God is the LORD (see chs. 6 and 7). Judgments create crisis. Crisis creates need. Need welcomes mercy, when God reveals his heart. And then it is that faith is born. But faith in what, particularly? That God himself provides the sacrifice for all Israel's sins—and by extension, the world's—and forgives Israel for all they have done, promising resurrection to the whole house of Israel (see ch. 6). Ezekiel's perspective is confirmed in the gospel by Paul in the book of Romans, which reveals Christ as the great sacrifice for all humanity. Judgments, therefore, lead to mercy. Ezekiel, though, has more to reveal.

His prophetic vision takes us into the final judgment with imagery almost identical to that in the book of Revelation (see ch. 7). He describes God's confrontation with Israel during the Babylonian invasion of that land hundreds of years before Christ. That confrontation is like "fire and brimstone." Yet, through it, Israel comes to know that God is the LORD. Thus, the Old Testament witness, along with the gospel in the New Testament, provides us with an understanding of the final judgment. It is not irreversible destruction. It is final reconciliation as God's glory meets human evil. It leads every knee to bow and every tongue to vow allegiance to the one on the throne, and to the Lamb, swearing that in him alone is their righteousness and strength.

Acknowledgments

I'M THANKFUL TO GOD, who, through his Son, made himself known to me as a teenager. That he has given me a life long enough to discover some of his ways and share them with the readers of this book is all thanks to his mercy to me.

I am indebted to the following great men of faith who, though they may not have believed in the salvation of all humanity (except, I believe, for Paul), nevertheless have influenced me deeply:

Paul, author of the Romans Letter that became the air I breathe; Augustine's *Confessions* disturbed and comforted me; Martin Luther's *Commentary on Galatians* gave me the muscle to wrestle with God; Anders Nygren's *Commentary on Romans* revealed the framework behind the book of Romans; Charles Hodge's commentary on Romans brought incisiveness to my writing; Karl Barth's *Epistle to the Romans* created unimaginable furrows in the mind; old Professor George Keough, Newbold College, England—I loved him, and the God he revealed; Professor Hans LaRondelle, Andrews University, Michigan—he made Romans live with the vibrancy of resurrection; Francis Schaeffer's lectures at L'Abri, Switzerland, made atheism impossible.

To the small band of my local radio and international podcast listeners also go my thanks. They have supported me and prayed over the writing of this book. Your faith has won out!

Certain friends should receive specific mention: my colleague and friend Tim Green, in England, who goaded me to write something substantial "for the wider believing public"; my friend Sharon Shull, who supplied the funds for a new laptop for me to work on the manuscript, regularly enquired how the writing was coming along, and prayed every day for it; Eric

Acknowledgments

Rasmussen, for generously keeping my computers buzzing and regularly helping me with my computer confusions; Nancy Knoll, for her friendship and faithful support of this ministry for many years; Jay Marcum, a generous supporter and friend who discussed aspects of the subject of this book during the writing of its early chapters; Tyler and Emily Herz, consistent supporters whose generosity and kindness are a gift of the Spirit; Eric Davis, who checked the accuracy of the verses, made helpful editorial suggestions, and bravely took on the task of creating a Scripture Index; Doug South, supporter and friend whose constant encouragement during my "writer frets" is a gift from heaven; Jerry Cramm, who saw early on the significance of what I was writing and regularly encouraged me.

I cannot say that everyone I have mentioned believes in the salvation of all humanity, but that they supported me in this endeavor shows their generosity of faith in Christ and their kindness of heart. Forgive me, I have an uncomfortable feeling I've left someone out. But thank you, too!

Lastly, I am thankful to David Block, a Christian brother, who, over coffee one day, handed me a booklet on the theme of the salvation of all humanity. His was the final nudge that led me to decide to start work on this glorious theme.

My book is for the concerned Christian layperson. Though it is more pastoral than academic, I have every expectation that many students, pastors, professors, and scholars will find their souls fed and their minds challenged and informed by it.

Nevertheless, I am indebted to several scholarly authors and their work on this subject. They have led the way. I'm thankful for their publications listed below, and for the light they have shone on the heart of God for all humanity:

Gregory MacDonald, *The Evangelical Universalist* (London: SPCK, 2012).

Thomas Talbott, *The Inescapable Love of God* (Eugene, OR: Cascade, 2014).

Jan Bonda, *The One Purpose of God* (Grand Rapids: Eerdmans, 1998).

Heath Bradley, *Flames of Love* (Eugene, OR: Wipf & Stock, 2012).

Bradley Jersak, *Her Gates Shall Never Be Shut* (Eugene, OR: Wipf & Stock, 2009).

Abbreviations

THE NEW KING JAMES Version of the Bible is the default version used for most of the texts quoted. In instances where I have used an alternative translation, its abbreviation is cited at the end of the verse reference. The full names of the Bibles quoted are listed below.

BSB	Berean Standard Bible
CEV	Contemporary English Version
CSB	Christian Standard Bible
ESV	English Standard Version
ISV	International Standard Version
KJV	King James Version
NASB	New American Standard Bible
NEB	New English Bible
NIV	New International Version
NKJV	New King James Version
NLT	New Living Translation
REV	Revised English Version
TLB	The Living Bible
WEY	Weymouth New Testament

Introduction

The Witness of Isaiah
God's Unbreakable Oath to All Humanity

FOR MANY YEARS I didn't take seriously several verses in the Bible's book of Isaiah that I now realize are so breathtaking you'd think they'd be up there competing with the Lord's Prayer or the Shepherd's psalm.

In these verses God speaks through the prophet declaring an oath he has taken, swearing by his own name, assuring us that his oath is backed up by his very own integrity, an oath so serious that God declares *it will never be revoked*—never repealed, never withdrawn—until its universal goal is accomplished. It is, therefore, an *unbreakable* oath. It will always be out there, reminding humanity of God's intention, and of his unswerving determination to see it through.

The World Is Given God's Irrevocable Oath

It would be perfectly reasonable, then, to expect God's followers to take serious notice of this oath. Yet it's baffling, let alone tragic, that the verses containing it hardly come up in Christian circles. And when on those rare occasions they do, almost universally, not-so-clever arguments are thrown up to neutralize their remarkable news. So, what aren't we getting?

Or is "getting it" problematic, since these verses simply don't fit how we think the final things of this world will work out and we're unwilling to face the creative tension between what we assume will happen in the end of time and what this oath says will *actually* happen? The oath I'm referring to is truly astonishing in its scope.

> Turn to me and be saved,
> *all the ends of the earth!*
> For I am God, and there is no other.
> By myself I have sworn;
> from my mouth has gone out in righteousness
> *a word that shall not return:*
> "To me every knee shall bow,
> every tongue shall swear allegiance."
> Only in the LORD, it shall be said of me,
> are righteousness and strength;
> to him shall come and be ashamed
> all who were incensed against him.
> (Isa 45:22–24 ESV)

Over seven hundred years before Christ, God sent these words out to the world through the prophet Isaiah. The Assyrian Empire had been swallowing up kingdom after kingdom around Judah (2 Kgs 19:17–18). Already it had wiped out ten of the tribes of Israel to the north, deporting its people to various parts of its empire (2 Kgs 17:16–23). And now it was Babylon's turn. They invaded Jerusalem to the south, destroying the temple, and removed thousands of the tribe of Judah from their land (2 Kgs 24:8—25:21). All seemed to flow from the chaos of raw power, and both Assyria and Babylon prided themselves in their conquests and boasted that their gods of wood and stone had brought them the victory.

But God sent messages through Isaiah that this was all his doing (2 Kgs 19:25). His sovereign power was using the nations to discipline his people (2 Kgs 17:5–8). Yet God would defend them and vindicate them and God himself before the nations (Isa 45:15–17, 25). Trouble was, that was far from how the nations saw it—if they'd heard Isaiah's message at all. To them Yahweh (Jehovah) was merely one of many local gods, and not noticeably powerful at that, since he'd appeared not even to have had strength enough to rescue Israel from its enemies (2 Kgs 17:24–33).

And then it was that God, in righteous indignation surely, proclaimed through Isaiah the most powerful redeeming news about himself found anywhere in the Old Testament, showing himself to be not one among many gods but the One and Only. "Before Me there was no god formed, nor shall there be after Me. I, even I am the LORD, *and beside Me there is no savior*" (Isa 43:10–11). "I am the LORD and there is no other; I form the light and create darkness, I make peace and create calamity" (Isa 45:6–7). "I have made the earth, and created man on it, I—My hands—stretched out the heavens, and all their host I have commanded" (Isa 45:12). Then, the breathtaking oath from the LORD (Yahweh). On the basis that "there is no other God" (Isa 45:14), he pronounces it. It is not a threat. It is an oath couched *in his victory and grace*. "Turn to me and be saved, *all the ends of the earth*! For I am God, and there is no other. By myself I have sworn; from my mouth has gone out in righteousness *a word that shall not return*: 'To me every knee shall bow, every tongue shall swear allegiance.'" Even those who have previously been angry with God will come to him and bow, and swear that in him alone is their righteousness and strength. There's a tone to God's oath that seems to say, "In spite of all the chaos among the nations, and the injustice inflicted upon the peoples, I, God alone, the creator of the heavens and the earth, will save." It is an *unconditional assurance* to all peoples of the world, for God is "a just God and a Savior" (Isa 45:21). The words "Look to Me, all you ends of the earth and be saved!" (Isa 45:22) express their universal reach. And they are more than an appeal. *They are an ingredient of the oath itself.*

For when God appeals for our response to his oath, he is initiating the process of turning that oath into reality in the hearts of men and women. God makes it clear in the next few verses that he will see to it that his appeal will become fact. That's when, a little later, he reminds the world of his authority and ability to accomplish what he intends: "I am God, and there is no other; I am God, and there is none like Me, declaring the end from the beginning . . . saying, 'My counsel shall stand, and *I will do all My pleasure*'" (Isa 46:9–10). Every knee *will bow*. Every tongue *will swear allegiance* to the LORD. The very content of the oath is a promissory note from God, assuring us that he can, and will, convince the world that justice and the strength to live dwell only in him, and finally all peoples—every knee and every tongue—will become persuaded of this, return to their right minds, and bow in devoted allegiance to him.

No sense of a tyrannical despot lingers here, as if God were saying, "I'll make you bow down to me, whether you like it or not!" The words flow from the owner of the earth who has glorious plans for it, and he has no intention of letting those plans fail: "Who formed the earth and made it, . . . Who did not create it in vain, Who formed it to be inhabited" (Isa 45:18). The forming of the world is God's gift to mankind and a further guarantee that his intentions will be fulfilled. Nor is there any room for the common, careless view that enemies who are mad at God are forcing through their teeth a reluctant acknowledgment, "Yes, we admit, you are God," before they meet their doom.

The ultimate bowing of all humanity is not about submission to power nor about submission to punishment, but surrender to an overwhelming conviction that God is *the redeeming Creator* (vv. 15, 18, 22). Everyone has been persuaded. They have now seen reality in the true light of God's presence. They are offering allegiance because they now comprehend that the Creator-Redeemer is the one source of righteousness and strength. Though many—perhaps most—of them were God's enemies, now, having seen things as they really are, they are ashamed.

His enemies' shame after their anger towards God is a *healing shame*, not a damning shame. That is clear in that the ashamed ones, being part of humanity, are among the "every knee" that bows and "every tongue" that swears, and therefore they take the same oath as the rest, an oath of life, swearing that in God is their sole source of life and wholeness.

Israel, who, through their history, reveal how God works with all the world, are also recorded as experiencing this healing shame when God's glory will be revealed, and he rises to forgive them for all they have done:

> And I will establish My covenant with you. Then you shall know that I am the LORD, that you may remember and be ashamed, and never open your mouth anymore because of your shame, when I provide you an atonement for all you have done, says the Lord GOD. (Ezek 16:62–63)

So, the shame is not a cry of despair pursuant to some dreadful end. It's the shame of humanity humbled to the core, who realize they were dreadfully wrong, who see now that God is the only Savior, and who are profoundly humbled to receive mercy. In fact, another of the psalmists prays for this shame to come upon the nations *so that they may search after God*:

> Fill their faces with shame,
> that they may seek Your name, O LORD.
> (Ps 83:16)

That shame is an aspect of faith that leads all who go through it to express that, after all, God alone is the source and center of their lives.

God's plan for his enemies is not that they submit *then perish*, but that they submit then enter into fellowship with him. The psalmist, centuries earlier, was aware of this redemptive process:

How awesome are Your works!
Through the greatness of Your power
Your enemies shall submit themselves to You.
All the earth shall worship You
and sing praises to You;
they shall sing praises to Your name.
(Ps 66:3–4)

God's Oath Shows the Purpose and Direction of Last Day Events

So, in the light of who it is declaring this oath—Almighty God, Creator and Redeemer of the heavens and the earth, before whom no other god exists, the one who is the Omnipotent, Omniscient, and Omnipresent one, who, in his emphatic sovereignty, declares "all souls are mine" (Ezek 18:4)—how can the oath he pronounced be understood as anything less than definitive? It declares his intention. It declares his plan. It declares the execution of his plan. And it declares its results. "So shall my word be that goes out from my mouth; it shall not return to me empty, but it shall accomplish that which I purpose, and shall succeed in the thing for which I sent it" (Isa 55:11 ESV). Clearly, God's oath is unbreakable. There are no ifs, ands, or buts. "The counsel of the LORD stands forever. The plans of His heart to all generations" (Ps 33:11). *In view of its absoluteness, is it not perfectly proper to say that all Scripture giving reference to the destiny of mankind must be interpreted in light of it?*

The Gospel Significance of God's Unbreakable Oath

> At the name of Jesus every knee will bow, of those who are *in heaven* [all angelic beings] and *on earth* [all living humanity] and *under the earth* [all the dead] and that *every tongue* will confess that Jesus Christ is Lord, to the glory of God the Father.
> (Phil 2:10–11 NASB)

Look at this! So significant is the irrevocable oath that the New Testament reveals it will be fulfilled through the gospel of Jesus Christ. That is to say, when the world sees—both here and in the final judgment—the full meaning of Christ's sacrifice for his creation, all hearts will be drawn to him and they will bow and swear allegiance to him—Jesus Christ. And that adoration of Christ, God's appointed Son, will involve *the whole universe from all ages of time*—those living in heaven, those alive on earth, and those "under" the earth, the dead.

How more far-reaching can it be expressed? The gospel, therefore, reveals the deep seriousness and universal nature of God's awesome oath. It promises that all God's creation will finally honor and glorify him—every last one of us—every last sheep *and goat*.

But when will this be? The final use of this verse is breathtaking. It nails it to the door of Christian pronouncements and should create reformation everywhere. The verse reveals that the fulfillment of God's irrevocable oath, when everyone will bow in allegiance before God and his Christ, will take place at *the final judgment*:

> For we shall all stand before *the judgment seat* of God. For it is written: "As I live, says the Lord, *every knee shall bow to Me, and every tongue shall confess to God*." (Rom 14:10–11)

God's Oath Calls for a Reexamination of Christian Assumptions

That Paul, in his Romans Letter, places the fulfillment of God's irrevocable oath in the time of the final judgment is of monumental significance. It should reengage all students of the Bible and all theologians, teachers, and preachers of Scripture in a serious reexamination of the direction and purpose of last-day events and the destiny of the world in the final judgment. The historical and pastoral failure to proclaim God's oath in relation to the gospel is a deep dishonor to God's grace for us in Jesus Christ, and to the humanity that desperately needs to hear it. For what we see here in the post-historical fulfillment of God's irrevocable oath in the final judgment is the wrapping up, or the commencement of the wrapping up, of the great conflict between good and evil. Its end goal is *the return of the world to God*, when knowledge of the LORD will cover the earth as the waters cover the sea (Isa 11:9).

This oath, remember, is the promise of God's victory of grace, winning ultimately the hearts and minds of all mankind. It is victory, grace, and irrevocable, unbreakable promise all rolled into one, when all creation finally, willingly, joyfully agrees that Christ alone is the righteousness and strength that God has provided for the whole of humanity.

Why, then, has God's oath, universal in its reach, unbreakable in its determination, spectacular in its goodwill to all humanity, been passed over, even hidden? What's behind this shunting to one side God's glorious commitment to the world? As a consequence of Christianity's disregard, God's irrevocable oath, resplendent with good news, is virtually unknown among the family of nations.

Alas, all is not cut and dried. We are met with a problem. Perhaps we've lacked the nerve to face it head on. And it's this: the final judgment described in the verses I have outlined *sounds very different in nature from the final judgment described in the book of Revelation.*

The Final Judgment: Does It Reconcile or Separate?

There, all the nations of the world are ranged against God's people—the saints—intent on wiping them out. But fire from God intervenes, destroying them all and saving his people. It's at this point, apparently, that the final judgment before the great white throne takes place and all, small and great, stand before God. Books are opened. And the Book of Life. All who are not found written in the Book of Life are cast into the lake of fire and brimstone. Then there follows a new heaven and a new earth (see Rev 20:7–15; 21:1).

Poles apart these two descriptions of the final judgment seem to be, wouldn't you say? The one is a description of an apparently blissful redemption of all; the other, a description of what appears to be a drastic redemption of the few. The one *uniting* the world; the other seeming to *rip it apart*. The one, saving all; the other, apparently destroying most, to save the few. The one making hell superfluous (for the lost are redeemed); the other appearing to make hell necessary (for the lost must be damned).

The presence of these two seemingly opposing visions of the final judgment in the Scriptures is one of the major reasons, I think, that most Christians have decided—whether they're aware of it or not—to stuff God's oath into a back corner, in view of our understanding of the final judgment in the book of Revelation. But this response should give us serious cause for alarm. *It implies a disturbing contentment on our part to settle for what appears to be a major contradiction in Scripture over the fundamental issue of humanity's final destiny.* Even though God swears by his irrevocable oath that every knee shall bow in allegiance to him, it appears that deeply hidden fears stemming from our understanding of the judgment of fire and brimstone in the book of Revelation have overwhelmed us, leaving us with no courage to explore how God brings his irrevocable oath to fulfillment in the light of that fire and brimstone judgment. Thus, we've produced for ourselves a false dilemma.

Historically, the church over the centuries slid into the paradigm of the final judgment as apparently described in the book of Revelation. Consequently, God's irrevocable oath almost everywhere in the Christian world has been treated *as if it were beneath serious consideration*. There's another word for that: *contempt*. Where discussion has come up on the subject at all, the rationalization has been put forward that one group of people will bow in worship, while the other group, hopelessly angry with God, will be forced to bow and then sent to eternal hell or be annihilated, even though the text, as we have seen, is against such an interpretation and makes it perfectly clear that both groups—*all* humanity; every tongue, every knee—will bow and take *a life-giving oath that the LORD alone is, and shall be, their fountain of life*. Beyond that, arguments slide even farther downhill.

The oath is conditional upon mankind's acceptance of it, it is said, which makes language meaningless. For if an oath is an oath and it cannot and will not be revoked—but then again, it will, if humanity does not agree to it—then what in the world are we talking about? Furthermore, whatever God says becomes impotent. His promises cannot be trusted because they all depend on humankind's deigning to accept them, and if mankind does not, then it is God who has to do the bowing—to the will of the world. The seriousness of God's words is then reduced to mere wishful thinking on his part, with no hope on God's earth of its ever being fulfilled.

Either–Or, or Both?

Are we left, then, with having to decide between one version of the final judgment over the other: either the irrevocable oath that God will finally bring all mankind under his loving sway, or the fires that destroy most of the world to bring peace to the few? Must we divide Scripture up and separate the New Testament judgment from the Old Testament oath? Or are there serious—and courageous—grounds for harmonizing these two seemingly different versions of the final judgment? And when it all comes down to it, does our decision depend on the deep feelings of those who legitimately believe the oppressors of the world need to face their monumental injustices, versus those whose equally deep concern for the disadvantaged leads them to believe the world hungers for heaps of mercy?

With the stark contrast of the two apparently contradictory ideas of final judgment in front of us, we become aware almost immediately of an involuntary *resistance* to the view that seems to shine the brightest with the surprise of God's grace. Those few verses containing God's irrevocable oath present a conflict for us. They appear to cut across everything we've previously known about God's ways.

Facing Emotional Prejudices

But instinctive reactions rise up precisely because our fears insist on keeping the two concepts of final judgment divided. That's when we set up one group of texts over against the oath, and blurt out objections like, "What about all the evil and injustice in the world perpetrated by people who deserve to be punished?" "What about all those people and nations who have rejected Christ?" "And 'the sheep and the goats'—what about them?"

Contradictions to our current, traditional thinking are, of course, unnerving. They threaten our settled reality. So, the brain frequently readjusts what appears to be irregular and reconstructs it in the mind's eye to harmonize with what we perceive reality *should* be. We do it more times than we think. But how about doing our Scripture homework instead? I'm not denying that some of my readers may have genuine biblical objections to the salvation of the whole human race, but the important thing to be aware of is that even genuine biblical objections are overlaid by the simple fact that we all have skin in the game.

And that skin in the game profoundly involves our personal emotions and experiences and loyalties. We are all stunted by guilt, shame, and fear in varying degrees. And we have all fled to our various closets of comfort as a result. The issues at hand are, therefore, not merely academic. No human being possesses total moral objectivity, including this writer. Many have experienced serious abuse and injustice, either on a deeply personal level or as puppets of political oppression. The prospect of seeing their abusers and persecutors forgiven and drawn into God's loving mercy presents to many a vision of outrage. Those oppressors need to be punished! But how about being punished *and forgiven*? Or does that rob us of our right to justice and vengeance? Does the gospel reveal a way to justice *and* mercy? We are faced, you see, with the nakedness of our souls. As Christians, we are called upon to be merciful to those who have persecuted us. Can we take this seriously all the way into the final judgment?

And what about the abusers and oppressors themselves, some who have abused individuals; others, massively on a global scale? When, in the final Judgement, the revelation hits them with full force and they see themselves as pitiful human beings who took on the mantle of terrifying power to hide their sociopathic weakness—all political stances now stripped away; wars, the terrifying extensions of ridiculous ego—will they be consumed to extinction by their shame? Or will they see in the distance the lingering light of God upon their twilight souls, raising them to a minimum of hope to receive mercy and forgiveness from God and from the masses stepping towards them, whom they have tortured—the masses who, against all instinct, have embraced Jesus devotedly enough to be willing to die a death to themselves in order to proffer freely the hand of forgiveness to their tormentors?

And are we not all guilty in one way or another, to one degree or another, and hiding shovelfuls of shame? Have we ever examined how that hidden guilt and shame leads us to interpret Scripture? Does our present psyche give us even the courage, let alone the mental tools, to read God's irrevocable, unbreakable oath as it stands, without an overwhelming surge of fear that news like that cannot possibly be *that* good—especially for *us*?

I submit that there's only one way to settle whether the final judgment is the fulfillment of God's irrevocable oath—that is, the reconciliation of all mankind to God—or the removal of the wicked from the earth by a lake drowning them endlessly in the pain of fire and brimstone.

And that is the gospel. It is the gospel alone that will give us the answer.

The Gospel Is Determinative

And by the gospel, I don't mean that "soft" gospel, which cherry picks to find only the pleasant verses that can be coated with a few spoonfuls of sugar to sweeten our delusions that "everybody's good at heart" and "God didn't make junk," or that "all religions lead to God." The irony is that Scripture's news about humanity is bad. Exceedingly bad. It is, in fact, catastrophic. But the news about the gospel is good beyond our wildest hopes and dreams. Half-baked interpretations of the gospel will never lead to the news that God can or will save all. The true, radical gospel, brimming with glory for humanity, is steeped in the blood, wrath, and sorrow of the loving heart of God.

How God brings every human being around, everywhere, in all epochs of time, to bow the knee adoringly before their Savior in the final judgment, how he skillfully persuades every tongue of its own free will to swear allegiance to him and sing his praise from a heart full of faith and gratitude, how he convinces all human beings—every last sheep *and goat*—to reconcile with their most painful enemies, is the greatest story ever told. Yet it is a story of the crisis of God whose heart, wrapped up in his Son's heart, is torn apart by the tragedy of the world. It is the drama of the ages, counterintuitive to all we know about human nature, the secret hidden from the beginning of time and finally made known through the gospel (Col 1:26–27). It is the story of the scandal of God (Gal 5:11) who acts towards mankind in ways utterly contrary to what we expect, the God who shocks and surprises us at every turn, the God who is both emotionally exhausting and spiritually exhilarating. The God who is at once an offense and a delight. He is altogether passionate love. But a love this great, a love that assaults our senses? A love that includes *and wins* everybody? Even the ones we find repulsive, the ones who've hurt us the most, the ones who've brought untold horror upon mankind? Yes, those too. Far from escaping the final judgment, they do indeed enter it and, by the very nature of its searing revelations in the presence of the Lamb, are brought to melting shame and an agonizing end of themselves, then to find their new beginning as sharers in the loving life of Christ.

Let's face it: if we're going to determine whether God's oath of reconciliation is the last word in the final judgment or if it's our *traditional* understanding of the fire and brimstone that settles it all, it's going to take the revelation of God's good news all over again, a revelation that makes our heads spin and our hearts melt. It certainly won't be business as usual.

When it comes to the things of God, was it ever?

Chapter 1

The Witness of Ephesians/Colossians

God's Secret Plan

> God has cherished in his own mind a secret plan since before time began. It's a plan that lines up perfectly with his merciful purpose, and he's going to put it into operation when the time is ripe. And here's the plan: to bring together the universe, everything in heaven and on earth, restoring the whole creation, into a unity in Christ as the Head.

THESE ARE NOT MY words. They are a composite of several translations of Ephesians chapter 1, verses 9 and 10. I put it together like this to break through that Scripture fatigue that often envelops us, leading us to slide over the meaning of a verse owing to our overfamiliarity with it.

Let me now quote several translations of these verses:

> ... when [God] made known to us the secret of His will. And this is in harmony with God's merciful purpose for the government of the world when the times are ripe for it—the purpose which He has cherished in His own mind of restoring the whole creation to find its one Head in Christ; yes, things in Heaven and things on earth, to find their one head in Him. (WEY)

> God has now revealed to us his mysterious will regarding Christ—which is to fulfill his own good plan. And this is the plan: At the right time he will bring everything together under the authority of Christ—everything in heaven and on earth. (NLT)

> He has made known to us His secret purpose—in accordance with the plan which He determined beforehand in Christ, to be put into effect when the time was ripe; namely, that the universe, everything in heaven and on earth, might be brought into a unity in Christ. (REV)

More Promises to Confirm God's Irrevocable Oath

Standing alone, these verses are extraordinary, revealing the breathtaking sweep of God's salvation plan for the universe. And when understood in the light of God's irrevocable oath that every knee shall bow and every tongue shall swear, they leap off the page. *Clearly, the apocalyptic destruction of the wicked and the redemption of the saved at the end of time is not, in fact, the climax of human history.* Rather, the pinnacle of God's intent, his secret plan that he's cherishing in his heart out of the sheer mercy of his nature, goes *beyond the apocalypse* to the "fullness of times" when the whole of human history, indeed, "the universe"—*everything* in heaven and on earth—will be "brought into a unity in Christ."

It seems highly likely that Paul had in mind God's unbreakable oath here when writing these words to the Ephesians since it forecasts the same universal outcome that God's oath promises, and since Paul already referred to that oath some time earlier when dictating his Romans Letter (Rom 14:11), and did so again, a couple of years later, when sending off his message to the Philippians (Phil 2:10–11).

Paul uses the word "mystery" to describe God's astonishingly magnificent intention, partly because God's loving heart is beyond our wildest dreams unless he reveals himself to us, and perhaps, as well, even when he does reveal his plan, we are too fearful to take it all in. Yet, it's not a mystery hidden forever but one that God takes great pleasure in gradually unveiling to us through his Son. But here we meet with our first pitfall. Given our human nature as it is, with so much deluded self-confidence, it's hard to avoid.

The Trap—The Illusion of Free Will

When we take on verses like these as confirmation that God will save everyone, there's a subtle trap waiting just a few steps ahead and that is the trivializing of this whole, awesome news by the assumption that mankind is actually *capable* of being saved—*savable*, one might say—that there's some part of it that has not been affected by sin—a divine spark, a god-link, perhaps—that can be recovered from the rest of humanity's mess. Perhaps people are not so bad in the end, basically good at heart. That popular saying "God didn't make junk" flows from what's called "creation theology"— that God made the first humans in his image, and consequently all will be saved based on that god-image quality within them.

Part of this humanistic reasoning involves the will. It's taken for granted among many Christians that everyone has the capacity of absolute free will and we're actually capable of using it to choose God or reject him. Salvation becomes something of a *decide* thing. A person can take it or leave it. This power of choice, it's assumed, is the savable part of a person. It's supposed we all stand at a crossroads in life as if we're in possession of the luxury of objectivity to decide which road to take, heaven or hell.

The assumption of absolute free will is so widespread, in fact, that both those who believe in the salvation of all and those who don't unconsciously use the same argument to make their case. Some Christians presume all will be saved because, well, who would be foolish enough to choose to go to hell and *not* to make a choice to go to heaven? Therefore, it's figured, all will choose it, and that settles it. On the other hand, more biblically based Christians conclude that since most of the world chooses not to accept Christ, they do, by default, choose of their absolute free will to go to hell instead. Thus, most will be lost. To a great extent, then, the question whether all or a few will be saved revolves around this naturalistic myth that we have the ability of absolute free will to choose for ourselves.

Humanity Trapped in Suppression of God

But enter the gospel. And at first, paradoxically, it appears to be far from good news. The facts, as the gospel describes them, confront us with a grim reality. All mankind, both pagan (Rom 1) and religious (Rom 2), is declared to be in a state of *suppression* of God (Rom 1:18). This deeply embedded denial of his presence and his loving involvement with mankind on a personal level is so persistent that it's unlikely we're consciously aware we're doing it. After all, when you suppress God you don't think about him. Yet the process is a mental and spiritual crisis of devastating proportions—a dynamic that humanity's history of cruelty and carnage bears witness to.

Men and women were originally made in God's image. To suppress God's presence is to deny our own being as creatures made with his image in us. It is to war, therefore, against our own souls. Humans were created with a natural bent to adore and enjoy their Creator. Childlike joy in him and worship of him were as natural as the air they breathed. They were carefree and safe, creative and satisfied. In his presence was "fullness of joy." At his right hand were "pleasures forevermore" (Ps 16:11).

But then entered that catastrophic event defining all history thereafter, the event described in the book of Genesis, when the first humans broke faith with God and ventured off on their own, only to bring about universal calamity.

It was the critical juncture in mankind's distant past when, far from *ascending* to a relationship with God, as social evolution would have us believe, humans did a *descent* from their innocent fellowship with their Creator, a complete separation from him, a nosedive into catastrophic spiritual alienation.

"With You is the fountain of life. In Your light we see light" (Ps 36:9). After that precipitous fall, the light went out in mankind. Only the terrifying void remained, *the dark mind* now staring back at them. Their thinking became meaningless. They "became futile in their thoughts" (Rom 1:21). Their emotions distorted, "their foolish hearts were darkened" (v. 21).

But because of the way we were created, the dark mind is psychologically intolerable to us. Desperate alternatives must be found. Mankind's passions, joys, longings, ecstasy—previously channels for the enjoyment of life in fellowship with their Father-Creator—*must* have somewhere to go.

Humanity's Alternatives to God

Yet mankind's reaction to their dark mind is utterly irrational. Instead of turning back to God, they did something parallel to insanity. Far from searching after God in order to return to him, humankind's guilt, shame, and fear drove them to "exchange him" for something else. The worship of images gradually evolved, images like the beasts and creeping things. And then, as time went on, men and women took to the madness of worshiping one another, desperately longing for human connection to fulfill spiritual needs—the worship of "the creature rather than the Creator" (Rom 1:25).

The lunacy and poignancy of this is beyond words. You hear the heart-cry of the soul, like the sound of the howling on a moonlit night, a cry that cannot be suppressed, rising from the gnawing pain over what is lost, yet finding no way to return to it. This is mankind's tragedy, their first sin after walking away from God. And it reveals that resolute drive in humanity to worship, a drive that cannot be ignored, for humans were *born* to worship the Lord. It is the life of the soul. Hence, humanity did not have the wherewithal to reject God outright, for then the terror of their total emptiness and darkness would utterly crush them. Rather, their only option was to *bend* and *contort* God in their darkened mind—to exchange him (see Rom 1:23) or substitute him for *a ghastly thing* by reducing the glory of the invisible God to idols, which gradually become paltry yet terrifying projections of their own distorted mind so that God is reduced to a mirror image of their broken self staring back at them with all the taunts they now feel in the depth of their soul. "Thus, they changed their glory into the image of an ox that eats grass" (Ps 106:20).

The game of fools had begun, stretching throughout humankind's tortuous history, the search for the delights and joys of the heart by the elevation of self to perverse godlike status.

In their attempts to reach this level, rituals develop. Magic arts, initiations, sacraments, sacrifices, and ceremonies abounded—the emergence of religion—all in a supposed search for the divine.

Religions: Humanity's *Flight from God*

Yet the gospel confronts us with the stark truth that mankind's religions, despite all appearances, are not a search for God but a *flight from him* (Rom 1:25). They flow from mankind's suppression of the true God—a replacement for the only glorious one who can now no longer be tolerated in the human psyche.

Here, then, is *religious humanity*. At the pinnacle of spiritual experience, they are actually in a descent into their own bottomless pit. At the pinnacle of spiritual experience, they reveal only *the sin of sanctimoniousness*, creating religious systems that exalt the human and produce only caricatures of God, systems that appear to relieve them of their shame but ultimately leave them emptier than ever of the sweet presence of their Father and Savior, and in possession now only of the irony of dread.

Religion is, consequently, the irresistible burden all humanity carries. It is the misfortune we are driven to, to thrust upon our empty souls. It is the obsession of the guilt-ridden. The terror of the devoted. The bearer of sad tidings. Religion cannot heal the human heart. It is the best mankind has to offer, yet it only exposes humanity's gaping wound. Religion is the poignantly beautiful art of the soul's indescribable void.

There remains for mankind only the putting away of their religion for the day in order to return to their secular, daily world where their emptiness now has been heightened by the judgments of their religion.

Now in their secular world, desperate escapes from the inner pain are needed, the inner pain which religion has served only to illuminate. Methods of escape multiply, as numerous as the desires of the heart—attempts to mimic the lost union with God who is now a distant, confused memory.

Religion and Escape: Addiction's Twins

Thus, religion and escape—religion and *addiction*, for addiction is an endless cycle of escapes from pain—go hand in hand. The one feeds the other. The more religion a person has, the more escapes they need. The more escapes, the more they must flee to religion for illusory relief—or at least bow to its terrifying demands. Their religious escapes create an endless vortex of destruction. And the irony is that their flight from God through religion and escapes only testifies, by its desperate denial, "that there is no other God besides Me, a just God and a Savior; there is none beside Me" (Isa 45:21). At best, religion can only make starkly real the void which Christ alone, when he is finally revealed, can fill.

Thus, sin is not, first off, a catalogue of various immoral acts, but a devastated state of mind in denial of its relationship to its loving Creator, and from which all sinful acts—as escapes—flow. Having pushed to the back of their thinking the one true lover and defender of their soul, there is nothing left to emerge from humankind's mental darkness but the dehumanizing of their being, which spawns all the sufferings of the world. Despots arise, godlike—*gross caricatures of humanity*—holding cruel sway over the oppressed. The obsession with self turns every innocent desire into a lust, clawing for godlike and godless fulfillment. Now, without our Creator-Father, self is center stage and spreads its idolatrous infection across the world.

Sin's Bondage

"*There is no difference*; for all have sinned and [continually] fall short of the glory of God" (Rom 3:22–23). We are now described as "without strength," "ungodly," "sinners," "enemies" (Rom 5:6, 8, 10). Our will has lost its free-acting capacity. "What I will to do, that I do not practice" (Rom 7:15). Even if we wanted to decide for God, we cannot. There is a strange fear pulling us away from the very God our souls need. And what God are we talking about, anyway? With the long, baleful history of so many idols of God our minds have created, who is the true God? (It is estimated that Hinduism alone has forty million gods!) Where now shall we find him? When Jesus expressed how hard it is for a rich man to enter heaven and his shocked followers blurted out, "Who then can be saved?" Jesus responded, "With men, this is impossible" (Matt 19:26). He could just as well have said this about all mankind. Humanity's suppression of God has now left them blind (Eph 4:18). They cannot decide because they cannot see. Created beings, desperately ruined, are now an impossibility, not a potential. Between God and humanity lies a great gulf which no human on earth can bridge.

If there were some exemplary people among us, it might provide a modicum of hope that one day we might reach their level—some moral heroes to guide us forward, perhaps, or groups from superior cultures or more enlightened civilizations, maybe. Or the educated who, by chance, might have attained elevated levels of perception and spirit. Surely some humble few might have what it takes to be saved? But no, "there is none righteous, no not one" (Rom 3:10). The history of religion is, alas, a history of pious confusion, war, and oppression. Even the "saints" have revealed searing moral and spiritual flaws, from Augustine, to Joan of Arc, to Mother Teresa, to modern-day preachers.

And the pathos in all this is that humans are not simply sinners anymore. They are "sold *under* sin" (Rom 7:14), a *slave* to it (Rom 6:17). The gospel calls it "bondage" (Rom 8:21). We moderns call it *addiction*. We passed mere sinning millennia ago. We don't do sin now. Sin *does* us. Humanity is under its "reign" (Rom 5:21). Sin has dominion over us. No longer having the luxury of choosing sin, *sin has chosen us*; we are its subjects (Rom 6:16). The insanity is within us. Its despotic rulership got us in its grip long ago. We were born into this kingdom as its slaves—and slaves are robbed of their freedom of choice. Each generation, one after another, has passed on its values, its traditions, *its darkness*, its behaviors, until we've become *victims of what we created*: sin, the oppressor. The slave has craved a master. And the slave master has smoothly obliged. And whoever now attempts to step out of line to reach the heights of morality and spiritual transcendence soon find themselves whipped back into line by the sheer moral torment of their demons and the drive of their passions, both of which pronounce them hypocrites and in chains—separated from the heart of the Father.

So it is that Paul's words ring true to what we know about ourselves when the lights are turned on: "Whatever the law says, it says to those who are under the law, that *every mouth* may be stopped, and *all the world* may become guilty before God" (Rom 3:19). Universal prisoners, then, of our own broken humanity—incapable of even desiring to be saved, incapable of even knowing what it is to be saved, incapable of *deciding* to be saved. Where is absolute free will here?

It's hard for any of us to swallow this. It's hard even to write it. We humans are a proud species. Pride is our reaction-formation against the tormenting, unconscious awareness that we are spiritually naked. So, we covet the cloak of self-respect and honor. We surround ourselves with the novel humanisms of the day, the motivational books and seminars backed up by feel-good, pseudo-Christian teaching which tell us we're all masterpieces of creation and need to realize our potential. We hear the regular and universal encouragements on countless graduation days, "Believe in yourself! You can become anything you choose to be!" We're swamped by the socio-technological—and yes, astonishing—achievements of the civilized world. And so, we revolt against these devastating biblical descriptions of the soul of mankind.

And yet the sheer reality of human nature forces us to admit what Scripture says. It is necessary to see things from God's point of view. The view of the "High and Lofty One Who inhabits eternity" (Isa 57:15), who "looks down from heaven upon the children of men, to see if there are any who understand, who seek God. They have all turned aside, they have together *become corrupt*. There is *none who does good*, no, not one" (Ps 14:2–3).

Salvation of All Impossible—If It's Up to Humans

Facing ourselves from God's vantage point, our "everybody's-good-at-heart" thinking scatters like ash before a breeze. When all is said and done, we see it as a product of our trivial minds. But then, enter fear. If mankind is so irretrievably sinful, so blind, so powerless, how in the world can God possibly gain the cooperation of mankind to save us all? The scriptural message of humanity's all-over-the-map corruption and the message of God's irrevocable oath clash like an irresistible force meeting an immovable object. This one fact leads most Christians to believe that the salvation of all is impossible. Maybe we started out believing that God will save everyone because we assumed humans are basically good. But we have ended up fearing that God *can't possibly* save everyone because we now see humans are basically bad. Our minds simply cannot bring the two antagonistic forces together. Doubt sneaks in and we slink back into thinking that perhaps God's irrevocable oath cannot be taken seriously after all.

Then it is that those other, long-misunderstood verses we find difficult to reconcile yet with God's oath come rushing in: the world of "the sheep and the goats," of "the saved and the lost," of "wailing and gnashing of teeth," of "believers and unbelievers," of the saints who "come out from among them and are separate," and the "wide and the narrow gate that leads to destruction." We shrink back: surely, it's just the few who will be saved, and the rest lost.

So quietly, sadly, we tuck away God's irrevocable oath again, almost with a whispered apology to God: "Sorry, God, I just can't believe it. How can it possibly be true? Your oath wasn't serious, was it? There's no way in the world it can happen."

Still, there remain those nudging, sweetly tormenting words of Jesus when he was talking to his disciples about the human impossibility of salvation. He didn't end there, did he? He went on to say, "But with God all things are possible" (Matt 19:26).

> He has made known to us His secret purpose—in accordance with the plan which He determined beforehand in Christ, to be put into effect when the time was ripe; namely, that the universe, everything in heaven and on earth, might be brought into a unity in Christ. (Eph 1:9–10 REV)

But how, Lord?

Chapter 2

The Witness of the Gospel (1)
God in Christ Carries the Judgment of the World

THERE'S A WORD PAUL uses in his Romans Letter that jolts the senses, once you realize what it means. The idea it suggests makes God seem offensive. Yet it was a word well-known to every Jew and gentile Paul was writing to, quite ho-hum to Roman citizens. The trouble is, Paul used this word *about God, the Creator of all humanity.*

He says that God presented Jesus to the world, as a *propitiation* by means of his death (Rom 3:25).

What is this word "propitiation"? It means to appease wrath or anger. And in the context Paul places it in above, he is saying that God presented Jesus to the world as the appeasement of his wrath by Jesus' death—a pagan-sounding idea, indeed. In fact, pagans in the Roman Empire used it quite commonly to describe the act of sprinkling incense on the public altars to appease any displeasure Caesar might have towards the citizens of Rome. Nothing too bizarre about that from their point of view. Pretty meaningless. Do it anyway. Who cares whether you believe or not? Those mad caesars considered themselves divine lords, and you don't want to mess with them. The Romans were no fools. They knew they weren't gods. But satisfy them—*propitiate them*—anyway, to keep the peace.

Propitiation, though, had a more serious meaning for people who really believed in their gods. They took the view that if the crops failed or there was an earthquake or volcanic eruption, or if a flood or drought blighted the land, it was a sign the gods were angry, and the way to handle these disasters, they thought, was to try to please their gods by offering sacrifices to lessen their anger, to make peace with them—that is, to appease or *propitiate* them. Sometimes the community priests would offer a pig or a goat, or something more substantial like a bull. And if the gods weren't impressed with that and the disasters kept coming, certain societies throughout history went so far as to offer the unthinkable—human sacrifice, babies and young virgins.

You can see from this that Paul's use of this word in reference to the true God, the Father-Creator of all mankind, through his Son, Jesus Christ, has been a deep embarrassment to many theologians and Bible translators. Some simply avoided translating the word into English altogether and used the word "expiation" instead. And of course, they constructed arguments for doing so, no matter how implausible. But that simply isn't the word Paul used. His word is propitiation, not expiation, a word perfectly understood, as I have noted, by every Roman. And it is a common rule of interpretation that a word must mean what it was understood to mean by those it was written to. Besides, there's a big difference between expiation and propitiation. Expiation refers to what God does for *mankind*—wipe out their sins. But propitiation refers to God, what he does for *himself*—appease his wrath.

So, what was Paul thinking, using a word like this? There must have been some serious force pushing him to do it, something, though incredibly offensive to human eyes, that was urging him to use it in relation to God.

And the fact is, there was. For propitiation is the most central truth of the gospel. Though it's a shock at first, it's *the major reason why we have all the liberty in the world to hope for the salvation of all humanity.*

And I must implore my readers to proceed slowly and carefully through the next few pages. And when you have done it, do it again! That Christ died for the sin of the world is known to all Christians. But *why* that had to be, and *what* it means to God, and *how* Christ's sacrifice has cancelled the eternal judgment of all humanity is the core of the gospel. It is the passionate driving force behind God's intension to rescue every last soul. And it is the ardent theme of every page of this book.

Here's the verse:

> Whom [referring to Jesus] God put forward as a *propitiation* by His blood to be received by faith. (Rom 3:25 ESV)

Here we have Paul saying that God put his Son, Jesus, on "display" (the word in the original language suggests this) in his death ("by His blood") *for all the world to see. And in his death, God's judgment (his wrath) upon all mankind was appeased and satisfied (propitiated). It was thus removed.*

Yes, it seems an offensive idea, doesn't it? But it won't do to brush it under the rug of our moral sensitivities. As I said at the beginning of this book, the gospel is the story of the scandal of God, who acts towards mankind in ways utterly contrary to what we would expect, the God who shocks and surprises us at every turn. The salvation of humankind presents a cosmic crisis for God, and no amount of theological papering over the cracks must be allowed to hide this fact.

By all that follows in the teaching of the Romans Letter, it's clear that propitiation reveals what the heart of God is like, what the sacrifice of Jesus does, and how the power of evil is crushed. God propitiates himself when his propitiation does its work. And then human beings are secure in his love, no matter how many crises God will yet take them through.

God Takes Humanity's Judgment on Himself

Notice, first of all, exactly what the verse says: "whom [referring to Jesus] *God* put forth." All that God does flows from love, and here we see his supreme act of love. It was God who put Jesus out there. It was God who provided the propitiation, *not humans*. "God so loved the world that *He* gave . . ." (John 3:16). In all pagan and false religions *humans themselves* attempt to appease God by giving their sacrifices. They try to make peace with God by their rituals and offerings and endless other ways of trying to please him. Desperate human initiative is at the heart of paganism. It is the source of all the supposed innate "spirituality" of humankind—the proliferation of human-centered religion. In clear-cut contrast to this, the gospel declares that it is *the God of love* who provides his own sacrifice. So, whatever it is that's going on in "propitiation," it's God doing it, not humans. He makes peace with himself—appeases his own wrath.

God's Wrathful Grief over the Ruin of the World

No matter how hard we try not to be, no matter how devoted to God we are, humans—Christians included—are infested with suspicions about God. A feeling that there is a dark side to God, a vindictive, mean streak in him, sneaks in during our unguarded moments. It's hard to shake, especially when we're engulfed in troubles or sins. In a more expansive way, we have to admit that at times, an unconscious sense surfaces that God is against humanity, only too eager to punish them and put an end to them. But the startling irony is, when propitiation is properly understood, God's wrath is the precise opposite of this.

Think of it this way and try to imagine God's mind: the fall of mankind, with all the evil, death, and unimaginable suffering it thrust forward in its wake, must be an infinite grief to our Creator. God is full of love, joy, passion. He is far from the unmoved mover that Aristotle contemplates or the God without passions that some theologians have imagined. He has the loving heart of an empowering father (Ps 103:13), the heart of a tender mother (Isa 49:15), the heart of a rapturous husband (Hos 2:19-20), and the joyful heart of a child (Matt 19:14), all rolled into one.

He loves taking care of the work of his hands. He "laid the foundations of the earth" (Ps 104:5). It's "full of [his] riches" (v. 24). He visits it and waters it (Ps 65:9) and "crowns the year with His goodness" (Ps 65:11). The fingerprints of his hand appear on all that's beautiful in the world: in the carpeted green of earth, the exotic sensuousness of spring, the gold embrace of warm light and lovers.

This God of ours is the love of which all other loves speak (see 1 John 4:7-8). He lightens the weary heart (Matt 11:28-30) and brings light and life and joy to humanity (see John 1:4, 9). He is the one whose lovingkindness "heals the brokenhearted," "comforts all who mourn," and gives a "garment of praise for the spirit of heaviness" (Isa 61:1-3). It is this God Most High who "is good to all, and His tender mercies are over all His works" (Ps 145:9). And, tragically, it's this God, and no other, whose love is unrequited by humanity's suppression of him from its universal consciousness (Rom 1:18).

If Scripture gives full acknowledgment to God's love for his creation—and it does—then, by that very fact it gives full recognition to the eternal grief and anger in his heart over the loss and suffering of that creation. Is it any wonder that he is "full of indignation" (Isa 30:27) as his love is scorned and he sees the murderous madness of mankind in one all-embracing glance? It doesn't take much imagination to feel God's hurt behind these words: "What injustice have your fathers found in Me, that they have gone far from Me, have followed idols, and have become idolaters?" (Jer 2:5). His pain must surely be inversely proportional to his heart of peace and love for all that is pure and good.

We humans find it impossible to grasp with any depth the *sorrow*, the *loss*, the *sense of injustice* that mankind's rejection of divine love has produced in God's heart. He is the eternal lover, spurned. We must try to comprehend that God is broken. Yes, he tells us exactly that. He is "broken over the whoring heart" of a world that has departed from him and gone after idols (Ezek 6:9 ESV).

And what if he were *unconcerned* about all this? What if he *had no loving wrath* in the presence of the evil and suffering mankind has heaped upon itself? That would be a horror too dreadful to contemplate. It would raise the terrifying specter of divine indifference towards the torments of humanity. Joy and pain would be the same to him. Life and death, too, and satisfaction and want. They would be met alike with all-knowing apathy. To us humans, that would mean the mockery of life's meaning. And the end would be our own extinction from the lack of a God who cares.

God's Wrath Motivated by His Love for Humanity

No, *God's wrath is real because God's love is real*. God's wrath is not against humans. God's wrath is passionately *for* humans because humans are against themselves and against the only source of their life. "It is to your own destruction, Israel, that you are against Me, against your help" (Hos 13:9 NASB). Humanity, therefore, is its own destroyer, and God's wrath is his loving determination not to allow mankind to fulfill its folly. "He who sins against Me wrongs his own soul; all those who hate Me love death" (Prov 8:36).

Consequently, when "the wrath of God is revealed," it's because of God's love for humanity. Our God is not merely "loving." Love is his very *essence* (1 John 4:8). Therefore, when God is wrathful, he does not suspend his love. His wrath is *motivated* by his love. Only a God who loves kindness can hate cruelty (see Amos 1:11–15). Only a God who delights in mercy finds vindictiveness loathsome (Amos 1:9). Our God who loves the beauty he has placed in the human heart feels wrath against the ugliness and cruelty that humans have created in its stead (Gen 6:5–6). Indeed, it's only the God who loves children who can say to those who harm them that he'll come upon them like a bear robbed of her cubs (Hos 13:8).

Hints of this loving wrath in the form of grief and anger appear in the heart of Jesus. Here he is, "meek and lowly in heart" (Matt 11:29 KJV) yet churning with "anger and distress" over the cruelty of one human to another (Mark 3:5)—precisely *because*, surely, of his love for them. This gentle Jesus who made everybody happy at a wedding party by making wine from water is described in the same chapter as making a whip from rope, overturning the money tables, and creating chaos in the temple because he was incensed that his Father's peaceful house was being turned into a market (John 2) and thus depriving people of a place to be loved. And it brings a lump to the throat when we see him standing by his friends, Mary and Martha, who are grieving over the death of their brother, and he is "groaning in His spirit and troubled" (John 11:33). The language in the original suggests snorting like a horse with anger. What else could this anger have been but his passionately loving heart in revolt against the sorrow that evil had brought into the world, of which the death of Lazarus was but one among billions and billions of tragic examples? And then there's that heartrending passage in the New Testament regarding Jesus' feminine-like grief for mankind in Matthew chapter 23, verse 37: "O Jerusalem, Jerusalem, the city that murders the prophets and stones the messengers sent to her! How often have I longed to gather your children, as a hen gathers her brood under her wings; but you would not let me" (REV). This is our gentle Jesus. And he who has seen Jesus has seen the heart of the Father (see John 14:9).

God's wrath, then—a love without equal in this world—is a state of indignation against the suffering that evil has brought upon the human family. And it is his determination to wipe it out from every corner of his universe and bring peace and joy back to humanity. We can hear in such wrath his pained cry for a creation that has become victim to forces leading the human race to turn upon itself and move dreadfully towards its own extinction.

There is a conflict, then, in God's heart of love. *Not a conflict of love and hate, where he loves one part of the human race and saves it, while hating the other part and predetermining its doom.* God is not divided. He is light, and with him there is no shadow of turning (Jas 1:17). Rather, the conflict is between *his love which desires to see righteousness in the world* and *his love which compassionately grieves for humanity's lostness*. We get a view of this conflict in God when it's described by the prophet in words that allude to an immense emotional upheaval in him:

> How can I give you up, O Ephraim? How can I surrender you, O Israel? How can I make you like Admah? How can I treat you like Zeboiim? *My heart is turned over within Me.* All My compassions are kindled. I will not execute My fierce anger; I will not destroy

Ephraim again. For I am God and not man, the Holy One in your midst, And I will not come in wrath. (Hos 11:8–9 NASB)

God Takes the Pain of Humanity

And here it is that we are confronted with the eternal love-drama of God's propitiation. Nothing like it has ever taken place before, and nothing similar to it will ever happen again. It is true that God the Father and Jesus sometimes compare their love with the love we have for our children and our spouses. But that is to give us a platform to leap from, into the arms of safety. There the comparison ends. In all the religions of the world, there is no historical precedent for the propitiatory love of God—*his own loving appeasement of his wrath against evil in order to save humanity*. And the Romans Letter does not compare but *contrasts* God's propitiatory love with the highest of human love:

> Scarcely for a righteous man will one die; yet perhaps for a good man someone would even dare to die. But God demonstrates His own love toward us, in that while we were still sinners, Christ died for us. (Rom 5:7–8)

The uniqueness of it creates a confusion in the human mind because logic could not have predicted it. No human yardstick can measure its value or significance; no parallels, illuminate its meaning. God's loving propitiation in taking his own wrath against sin goes beyond describing the apex of human history. It *defines* history itself by determining its meaning, its course, and its ultimate destination. Our confusion leads to a sense of the scandal of it. "And he will startle many nations. Kings will stand speechless in his presence. For they will see what they had not been told; they will understand what they had not heard about" (Isa 52:15 TLB). The rest of mankind at best re-scrambles their brains to come up with the assessment that it is all so much foolishness (see 1 Cor 1:18–25).

God enters the world.

As man. Born a man. "He was manifested in the flesh" (1 Tim 3:16). "In the beginning was the Word, . . . and the Word was God. . . . And the Word became flesh and dwelt among us" (John 1:1–2, 14). The Creator did not simply appear as a man. He was *incarnated* a man, entering the world through the birth canal of his human mother. And though without sin, he allowed himself to be sucked in to the riptide of evil, just as mankind has been. "God [the Father] made Him [God, the Son] who knew no sin, to be sin for us" (2 Cor 5:21).

> Surely He has borne our griefs
> And carried our sorrows. . . .
> He was wounded for our transgressions,
> He was bruised for our iniquities. . . .
> And the LORD has laid on Him the iniquity of us all.
> (Isa 53:4–6)

And so, Jesus was crucified. Crucified, yes, but it was not the crucifying that finally took him. That slow death would have lasted anywhere from three to five days, his vital forces slowly draining out of his agonized body—lockjaw, hallucinations, dehydration, asphyxiation, and unimaginable physical pain—until his frame would have been no longer able to sustain it and life's final wisps would have drifted weightless away. But Jesus died after only six hours on the cross. Not because of anything less horrific than crucifixion but because of something infinitely more terrible.

Even the night before in the garden of Gethsemane, the horror launched its assault on his soul as Jesus "began to be full of terror and distress" (Mark 14:33 WEY). "My heart is ready to break with grief," he said (Mark 14:34 NEB). The Message (a paraphrase of the Bible) here reads, Jesus "sank into a sinkhole of dreadful agony." The words in the original language are so strong as to suggest he would have died right there in the garden if an angel had not been sent to strengthen him (Luke 22:43).

The horror climaxed on the cross the next day with untempered force when Jesus cried that eternal wail of sorrow: "My God, My God, why have You forsaken Me?" (Matt 27:46). He who had always known his Father more intimately that any human born, whose gaze was always turned towards the inexpressible light of God's beauty, was now alone, folded only in the torment of darkness and abandonment—and sin.

This scene has often been treated with witless simplicity. It's been thought that this gentle Jesus was facing a cruel, hard judge of a Father. But Jesus was not anything less than God himself, the Second Person of the Godhead. Jesus is "the exact imprint of [God's] nature" (Heb 1:3 ESV). All that the Son knows and experiences, the Father knows and experiences. "I and My Father are One," he said (John 10:30). Thus, what Jesus was suffering on the cross, the Father was suffering with equal intensity.

The Witness of the Gospel (1)

God's Self-Abandonment to Rescue the World

So, it was God-become-man who carried the calamity of mankind, and the pain of humanity's aborted love for him, in the person of God's Son. In the cry "My God, why have your forsaken Me?" is the cry of *God separated from God*. It is the cry of the broken heart. In some mysterious way which we can hardly begin to glimpse, there was a seeming split in the Trinity. *God abandoned himself* on the cross. Like a father who abandons his own life to save his child from an impending disaster, *God* abandoned *God* to save us. He abandoned himself to evil, and to the darkness of separation from his own glorious presence. God in heaven was suffering the horror of what God on earth was suffering. Jesus, God-among-humanity, died—after those six dreadful hours of the grief of being separated from God, his Father. In some unfathomably mysterious way, God died of the grief of self-abandonment. And God abandoned himself *that the human race may never be abandoned*.

Don't give up, I say to you, my reader, in stretching your mind to understand this. There is more. It is this reality beyond any other—God's abandonment of himself for us—that assures us of his plan to rescue the whole human family. No single person, even in the most obscure, piddling place on earth, will ever be forgotten.

Thus astonishingly, God brought himself to peace by taking the insanity of the world upon himself. *He who knew no sin became sin for us. He bore our griefs and carried our sorrows and iniquities.*

In the full light of the final judgment we shall be *engulfed* by the wonder of all this. It is presently beyond the human mind to take in. Yet we must try.

What is it to "bear," to "carry," and to be "bruised" for these horrors of the soul?

True love identifies in every detail with the one loved. And certainly Jesus, in his divine love for human beings, carried our griefs and sorrows in that way, until his soul ached with indescribable pain as if all our sin and dying were his. In this, we, who believe, know that our heaviness doesn't drag along with it the added weight of guilt, shame, and the fear of the ultimate death. Though we still suffer the effects of sin and death in the world, we know that the *condemnation*—the *judgment*—for it has been carried by Jesus, the Messiah of the world.

God-in-Christ: The Offense

But it goes beyond that. It is not enough to say that Jesus carried our sins in the sense of taking the blame upon himself. Jesus was blamed. He didn't simply take the blame. He was *blamed by the Jews. Blamed by the Romans. Blamed by all the world.* Jesus, as the God-man, is accused by global mob mentality. He stands condemned. He hangs, executed. In the Pharisees, in the Jews, in the Romans is epitomized the attitude of all humanity in arrogant judgment of God. Mankind is the accuser. Mankind, the judge. Mankind, the executioner—*of God.* He who "made himself of no reputation" (Phil 2:7) came to be thought of as "stricken and smitten" justly—*by God* (see Isa 53:4).

And so, Jesus, the one "who knew no sin and becomes sin for us," is charged, found guilty, and executed for the evil of the world's history. He is the one in the dock. He never stood a chance. A universal consciousness of God-resistance had made up its mind before ever the facts were known. Upon him falls humanity's accumulated anger against its suffering and injustice. He receives the world's indictment for being the dictator, the tyrant, the abuser who oppresses all his creatures. He is blamed as the originator of psychic torment, the one who causes the inconceivable emptiness in the souls of a billion and more addicted human beings. Here he is, appearing to accuse all the innocent and helpless on earth when they hadn't a chance to be any different, the one leader of human trafficking because he did not come to the aid of the victims to set them free. This is the God who made the earth bent on creating earthquakes, volcanic eruptions, and tsunamis that toss humans and their homes about like toys. Every time an abused soul cries out—"Why, God?!"—*there,* in microcosm, is the accusation of all humanity, and God stands accused and condemned. When a young Indian school girl is raped, disemboweled, and thrown off a bus by a gang of boys, in her final sobs one hears the heart's despair, "Where were you, God?" and God stands accused and condemned. As a little boy in Yemen falls upon his father killed by a bomb at a wedding party—embracing him and pleading, "Daddy! Wake up!"—God stands accused and condemned. Starving people in distant lands, no longer able to eke out the last smidgen of life for lack of bread, release their final sighs of incrimination against the Most High. Millions of naked souls shambling, wary, into the gas showers, only to be removed as congealed human heaps after the final screams fade, testify against God, "Why did you abandon your chosen people?" The ten million street children in India sleeping on cardboard in train stations and under bridges cry out to an absent Father-God. Untold multitudes of babies snuffed out before they saw the light of day become the ultimate statement, "We are the 'not-beloved' of the Creator" (see Rom 9:25).

Is it fair to say that God is blamed for these harrowing human situations? How can it mean anything less if we believe God "became sin" for us in Christ, *taking* the blame and *being* blamed for all the evil that has befallen this planet? "Why, God?" "Where are you, God?" "Why me, God?" "How could you let this happen, God?" "There is no God!" These are humanity's wails of grief against their Creator. God cannot be sanitized. The romanticization of the cross is a callous ugliness. God does not escape the world's insufferable grime. He is part of it. "He dwelt among us." "He came to His own and His own did not receive Him" (John 1:11). *He appears not to have accomplished what he had promised.* "He was despised and rejected by men, a man of sorrows and acquainted with grief" (Isa 53:3). *And the cross still mocks him as weak and a failure. His very way of saving humanity was the reason why they abandoned him.* He becomes the world's disappointment. He stands before us as "mission aborted." His moment of absurdity, the occasion of his incomprehensible insanity. His foolishness is our embarrassment. He is what he said he was all along: "a stumbling stone and a rock of offense" (Rom 9:33).

How can we wrap our minds around this bizarre act of God in the suffering Christ? Who can believe such a report (see Isa 53:1)? How can his taking on the world's lunacy possibly propitiate *him* and give *us* hope?

When God took the world's judgment upon himself in the person of his Son, he launched his heart's desire—the process of drawing the whole world back into his yearning heart.

Christ Reconciles the World to God

> God was *in Christ reconciling the world to Himself*, not counting their trespasses against them. (2 Cor 5:19 NASB)

The *world*, you notice. Not a mere part of it. We must learn to see *how* God's propitiatory act reconciles the world to himself. For the start it must be seen that in the dying of God for mankind—this act of meek, wrathful love—is the commencement of that plan described in Ephesians: that "He might gather together in one all things in Christ, both which are in heaven and which are on earth" (Eph 1:10). And as all is accomplished through this beyond-history-defining-history act of love, he views the future and "shall see the labor of His soul *and be satisfied*" (Isa 53:11). Satisfied? Yes, *appeased, propitiated*—satisfied.

No greater satisfaction does God enjoy than *loving*. "He delights in mercy" (Mic 7:18). It is his heart in action. And no greater loving happened than when God, in Christ, took his wrath against the sin of mankind and suffered its judgment himself—the judgment and death of the world—in order to rescue it, bring it to life, and pull it back into his embrace.

"It pleased the LORD to bruise Him[-self]" (because it was God in the person of Jesus who put himself under the judgment of death). He put *himself* to grief (see Isa 53:10). When he did this, he made himself an offering for sin (Isa 53:10)—the sin of the world. "Behold the Lamb of God *who takes away the sin of the world*" (John 1:29). In this one propitiatory act of loving wrath, God in Christ was pleased to suffer for the sake of removing eternal judgment from every person in the world. It was a lonely, violent act of love in which God stood in for mankind and "removed the iniquity of that land in one day" (Zech 3:9).

So astonishing a sacrifice God made, unique in time and eternity, that Paul in his Romans Letter spends nine of his sixteen chapters describing what it means. And in the middle of it all it seems that his heart almost bursts as his contemplation climaxes, realizing what God's loving propitiation has pulled off. What God has done in Christ persuades Paul, *convinces* him, that God's love has conquered *all* and *all things*.

Christ Removes All Barriers Between God and Mankind

> I am persuaded that neither death nor life, nor angels nor principalities nor powers, nor things present nor things to come, nor height nor depth, nor any other created thing, shall be able to separate us from the love of God, which is in Christ Jesus our Lord. (Rom 8:38–39)

Invincible love is being described here, irresistible love that no power in heaven or earth can separate from its object—love that is the power of God, that finally overwhelms the human mind and irresistibly *compels* and *draws* the heart and will by the lavishness of it. God knows what he is doing by such humanly baffling love. He knows that his love has conquered—conquered all evil, all sin, all doubt, all death. This is triumphant love. It reaches beyond *death*, breaking down its awful, separating barrier. Nor is there anything in all of *life's* tragedies, sufferings, sin, and disorder that can stop it. Not even the *powers* of world governments or demonic *principalities* can hold it back. No calamities of the *present* nor anxieties over the *future* can choke off this love. Nothing in the *heights* of knowledge beyond us nor anything in the *depths* of sorrow, depression, or unmastered despair can divert the flow of God's saving love towards us. There is, emphatically, *no created thing*—sins and doubts, wars, calamities, despair and death, even unbelief—that can impede the victory of God's irrepressible love from winning his creation back into his heart.

Yes, for sure, present reality and mankind's attitude towards God-in-Christ appear to make this claim seem nothing short of absurd. Where do we see God's sacrificial love bringing the world to a screeching halt? As things stand, it's not looking good for God. Humanity thinks little of his love. Love, after all, is not the coin of this realm—sadly, not even among many Christians. Power, yes, political and financial. Social image, prestige. Victories—God-forbid we should suffer defeat! That's what mankind knows. Love stands little chance of making a dent. Leave it for our personal, spiritual moments because it appears it will do little to alter the course of the world. It seems far easier to expect that the few will be saved and the rest of humanity will face its doom than to expect what would seem to be castle-in-the-air salvation of all his creation.

But what appears to be God's irrelevance—or worse still, the outrageous relevance of God's apparent absconding—is, paradoxically, his power. For "the foolishness of God is wiser than men and the *weakness* of God is *stronger* than men" (1 Cor 1:25).

Christ Will Draw All Humanity to Himself

Along with Paul's words, "God was in Christ reconciling the world to Himself," Jesus himself made this emphatic declaration:

> "Now is the judgment of this world; now will the ruler of this world be cast out. And I, when I am lifted up from the earth, will draw all people to myself." He said this to show by what kind of death he was going to die. (John 12:32–33 ESV).

Here, these verses show that the world's eternal judgment is taken by the one man standing in for, and representing, all humanity. When God in Christ takes eternal judgment upon himself instead of letting humanity suffer it, by that supreme act he will ultimately *draw* and *persuade* all human beings to himself. Though countless millions have been drawn to the love of God in Christ over the centuries, we have not yet seen "all" drawn to him.

But the prophet John peers into the future, and we see Christ's sacrifice stretching its drawing power right into eternity and the final judgment.

The Sacrificial Lamb: The Foundation of the Final Judgment

> Behold, in the midst of the throne . . . stood *a Lamb as though it had been slain.* . . . *And every creature which is in heaven and on the earth and under the earth and such as are in the sea, and all that are in them* [who is left?], I heard saying: "Blessing and honor and glory and power be to *Him who sits on the throne*, and to *the Lamb*, forever and ever!" (Rev 5:6, 13)

In this highly symbolic language, Christ the Savior is presented as a Lamb. And, astonishingly, he appears on the throne of God not in his resurrected state, but still as though he had been slain. This is a clear statement that *the final word in the governance of God's kingdom is sacrificial mercy*—the merciful love of God's sacrificial act of taking the judgment of the world upon himself in Christ, the Lamb, *a Lamb as though it had been slain*. "In mercy the throne will be established" (Isa 16:5). And all mankind—every creature which is in heaven and on the earth and under the earth and such as are in the sea, and all that are in them—are drawn to adoration and worship because of it. "You are worthy . . . for You were slain" (Rev 5:9). And thus, Christ's "lifting up" on the cross—even the "lifting up" of the cross stretching right into the final judgment—ultimately draws "all"—all his creation—back to himself.

Other passages in the Bible describe this picture of universal accord and praise to God rising from every one of God's creatures. We have already seen that God's irrevocable oath, recorded in Isaiah, promises that every knee will bow, and every tongue will swear allegiance to the LORD, their righteousness and strength (Isa 45:22–24).

We saw, too, in Romans that it will be at the final judgment that every knee bows and every tongue swears allegiance to Christ (Rom 14:10–11).

And then we learned that moment is predicted in the book of Ephesians when God's purpose, the secret of his will, is ready for its unveiling when the time is ripe: "*that the universe, everything in heaven and on earth*, might be brought into a unity in Christ" (Eph 1:10 REV).

And now, here, in the book of Revelation, the same scene is described when all creatures in heaven and all the creatures on earth and all the dead "under the earth" burst out with cheers and joy and praise to God and the Lamb. The joy is so resoundingly expansive that John, who describes this scene, cannot resist interpreting even the frenzied frolicking of all the sea creatures as praise to the sacrificial love of God. Thus, the whole universe becomes a magnificent theater of cavernous praise to God and the Lamb.

So, it is *irresistible* love, a love overwhelming by the drawing power of the uplifted Christ. Here is our certainty for the salvation of all mankind. For the judgment that belonged to us has been taken by the supreme love of God himself, making way for the universe—everything in heaven and on earth and under the earth—to be drawn into a joyful unity in Christ.

The Doubters with the "If" Conditions

Ah, but nevertheless—that abysmal nevertheless—nevertheless, in the blink of an eye, the majesty, the awe, the thrill of this good news can be stolen away by one seemingly innocent statement:

"Yes, true, but of course, people have to accept it."

Or, "Yes, true . . . *if* people have faith, you mean, right?"

"But people have to make a choice, don't they?"

And the implication flows from these statements that the victory of God's love can be no victory at all if mankind does not choose by faith to accept it. And, knowing human nature, we know where that leads.

The issue of how faith enters the mix and what part it plays is a major theme of this book. The urge is naturally strong at this point to press the issue, "But what about faith!" It is a vital question, and I will not sidestep it.

But for the present it must be said that if the choice to believe is the initiative of human beings, then it is humans who are the arbiters, who determine whether God's love is finally triumphant or not, and thus, God's "invincible" love becomes no stronger than the weakest faith that believes it—or doubts it. And since, it is *assumed*, most people will choose not to believe it, then God's invincible love will not finally win. It is then that God's love becomes no more than pathos. And God is to be most pitied. For he will have loved with indescribable and terribly pained love—*and lost*. He will have sacrificed himself and, in spite of it, saved some while watching the majority of his children slide into the horrors of oblivion. In that case, evil will have secured multitudes more children for hell than God will have gained for heaven. Evil's hatred will have bested God's love. And thus, God will have become the poignant exhibit of eternal tragedy.

But God's love is *not* pathos. It is triumphant joy. There is enough pathos in Christian culture to paint the planet with it. And it never dries. It clings at the least touch to our mournful souls, gradually disfiguring our love into an ugly obsession with self-pity.

But God's love in the end triumphs over self-pity and sorrow. It fills the universe with praise for his victorious grace. He alone is the Savior. There is none besides him (see Isa 45:21). Every tongue takes up the strain that in him alone the whole world finds its righteousness and strength. And the Lord will make bare his holy arm "in the eyes of all the nations: and all the ends of the earth shall see the salvation of our God" (Isa 52:10).

Chapter 3

The Witness of the Gospel (2)
Christ's Redemption Equal
in Extent to Adam's Fall

THERE'S A WHOLE HIMALAYAN range of spiritual perspectives in Paul's Romans Letter, summit peaks that provide breathtaking vistas of the depths, breadth, and heights of God's grace to mankind. One of those majestic views—some may consider it the one that tops them all—describes the history of the salvation of all the world.

So distinct is this vista, so seemingly different from anything Paul had laid out in the earlier chapters of his letter, that some theologians have assumed Paul went off on a tangent before yanking himself back and resuming his theme in chapter 6 of the letter. The passage appears to them to have no context, no connection with what he'd said before or with what he follows on with after.

But other theologians, who, as I see it, have captured Paul's thought process more accurately, have believed that his tangent was no tangent at all, but the logical summit that his previous thoughts and arguments were reaching towards, until he finally breaks through the clouds into the sunlit pinnacle of what Christ means for the whole world.

The passage I'm referring to specifically is Romans chapter 5, verses 12 to 21. It's lengthy. So, I'll attempt to take it apart first. And let me say, we'll need to put our working boots on here. It's not going to be a walk in the park. Yet when we reach the peak of Paul's thoughts, we'll be exhilarated by the vista stretching before us.

Paul begins by saying, "Sin came into the world through one man" (v. 12). And, of course, he's referring to Adam. But he doesn't *exactly* say that. He says, "*Just as* sin came into the world through one man..." Just as? Paul's about to make a comparison. With what? With whom?

With Christ. "... Adam, who is a type of Him who was to come" (v. 14).

It's difficult to convey the highly charged nature of Paul's statement here. Its implications are breathtaking. Adam brought ruin. Christ brought redemption. Adam brought sin. Christ brought righteousness. Adam brought death. Christ brought life. How can the one possibly be a type (a resemblance, a sample) of the other?

And yet Paul is so at pains to convey this parallel between Adam and Christ that he spends the next seven verses describing it repeatedly. And more, even though Paul fully acknowledges the opposite influence of Adam's and Christ's lives, he persists in paralleling even their opposites. What is going on here that is so vital that Paul strains to show the *resemblance* of Adam to Christ even through their *contrasts*? First, he says, "The gift is not like the offense" (v. 15)—meaning, the gift that Christ brought to the world is not like the sin that Adam brought to the world. Nevertheless, Paul pushes through in portraying the one as a type of the other. Again, he says, "The gift is not like that which came through the one who sinned" (v. 16). Yet, for the rest of the chapter he plows ahead demonstrating their equivalence.

Why would he so adamantly pursue this paradoxical idea? He could just as easily have said, "Even though Adam brought in all this sin and death, thank God Christ brought us redemption." Yet beyond pointing out that Adam represented everything bad that came into the world ("Just as through one man sin entered the world, and death through sin..." [v. 12]) while Christ represents everything good that came into the world ("even so grace... through righteousness to eternal life through Jesus Christ" [v. 21]), he's on to something deeper that leads him to assert, in effect, that *Adam's evil is a mirror image of Christ's good.*

Now, lest you're in any doubt that he does this, follow the verses below and note how Paul parallels the contrasts. They stand out like glowworms in the night.

> If many died through one man's trespass... *much more*... the grace... of that one man... Christ, abounded for many.
> (v. 15 ESV)

> The judgment following one trespass brought condemnation, but *the free gift following many trespasses brought justification.*
> (v. 16 ESV)

> If, because of one man's trespass, death reigned . . . , *much more [those receiving] . . . the free gift of righteousness reign in life.*
> (v. 17 ESV)

> As one [man's] trespass led to condemnation for all men, *so [one man's righteous act] leads to justification and life for all men.*
> (v. 18 ESV)

> As by the one man's disobedience the many were made sinners, *so by the one man's obedience the many will be made righteous.*
> (v. 19 ESV)

> As sin reigned in death, *grace also might also reign through righteousness . . . to eternal life.*
> (v. 21 ESV)

So, then, that Paul compares Adam with Christ in some way is clear. What takes a little more digging is, *Why is he comparing them? And what is he comparing? What is it about Adam that makes him a type of Christ?* To strain the language, and even our powers of thought, must mean there's something eminently important in Paul's paralleling of the two great monoliths of history.

A Comparison of Opposites

And indeed, there is. *And it's one of those core issues of the gospel that display God's intention to save all mankind.* There are two ways revealed in the passage in which Adam is a type of Christ.

The first is this: "Through one man sin entered the world and death through sin" (v. 12), and "death reigned," Paul says, *"even over those who had not sinned according to the likeness of the transgression of Adam, who is a type"* (Rom 5:14). So, Adam brought something into the world—sin and death—and the whole world suffered from it, even though humanity after Adam did not cause it. From Adam's sin, in which the world had no part, condemnation and death came upon all humanity. Even though we're all sinners in our own right, we nevertheless find ourselves *victims of someone else's wrongdoing* (Adam's) the moment we enter the world.

In the same way, "through one man's righteous act the free gift came to all" (v. 18). So, Christ also brought something into the world—righteousness and life—and the whole world benefits from it, even though humanity after Christ did not cause it. From Christ's righteous life, in which the world also had no part, justification and life come upon all humanity. Even though we're all sinners in our own right, we nevertheless find ourselves *recipients* of someone else's goodness (Christ's) the moment we enter the world.

So, as with justification—it comes to the world also as a *gift* (see vv. 16, 18) and mankind plays no part in it—so with righteousness in Christ—it comes to the world as a gift (v. 17), and it does not come from human accomplishment. And as with obedience—as by one man's disobedience mankind was made sinful (v. 19) by no fault of its own—so also mankind will be made righteous by no cause coming from itself (v. 19). And it's the same with eternal life. It comes to humanity through the grace that comes through Jesus Christ—not by mankind's evolutionary development, biological engineering, or universal transcendence.

So, this is the first part of the type: humanity participates in Adam's sin, *in which it had no part* just as humanity participates in Christ's righteousness *in which it had no part*. Adam brought a "gift" of condemnation and death. Christ brought a gift of justification and life. What an incredible God to counter everything that evil has brought in through the grace of Christ! We will see, after a few more pages, how Paul arrives at this awesome conclusion. But for the present, there's more to explore in the comparison of Adam to Christ.

A Comparison of Similarities

If Paul's first comparison between Adam and Christ shows the heights of God's grace to us, his second comparison shows its awesome breadth. The first part of the type, as magnificent as it is, isn't sufficient to fill out the meaning of Paul's thought completely. There's something more, something beyond what he's already reached for. He's not at the summit of his argument yet. But he's about to break through. Since Adam's being a type of Christ does not reside, as we have seen, in the *kinds* of lives Adam and Christ passed on (because Adam handed down sin, but Christ handed down goodness), the comparison must be something else. And the clue is how Paul makes use of the fact of "many" and "all," speaking of the mass of people who are affected by Adam's sin and Christ's righteousness.

The Witness of the Gospel (2)

What we'll see shortly is that it's not the kinds of influence that Adam and Christ had on the world that are paralleled, but the *extent* of their influence that's being compared. Paul equates not the worth of Adam's life with Christ's life, *but the universal effect that both lives have on humanity. This is the second part of the type*. And it is this second part of the type that most theologians hesitate to draw logical conclusions from because their presupposition that God will save the few while the majority will be lost does not fit the type that Paul is describing.

Paul, as if to provide his readers with some form or comparison to understand how far-reaching Christ's salvation is, employs Adam as a measuring rod. It's a clever means of measurement. What happens to Adam—sin and death—happens to *everybody*. All of Paul's readers, Jew, Christian, and gentile, would instinctively comprehend the blanket impact of sin and death on every human being without distinction simply by their own experience—at the very least, from their common familiarity with death, "for the living know that they will die" (Eccl 9:5). Hence, the Adam-yardstick.

Just below, therefore, is a layout of the verses of this passage, making clear how Paul is comparing the universal impact of Adam's life with the same extensive, universal impact of Christ's life. What went on with Adam happens to all the world. What went on with Christ, in due time, *also happens to all the world*.

> Verse 15: As many died (obviously meaning "all," since all die) from Adam's offense, the same "many" (the "all" who died) receive the grace abounding.
>
> As the judgment from sin brought condemnation—obviously to all, since all are under sin (Rom 3:9)—so the gift results in justification—obviously also to all, since the justification is to the "all" who are under condemnation (v. 16). And since it is not condemnation and justification that are parallel, what else can be parallel but the *extent* he's referring to by the use of "many" and later "all"?
>
> Verse 17: As death reigns—obviously over all, since all die—so life through Christ reigns—obviously over all, since Paul is talking about the all who are under the reign of death. And since death and life are not parallel, to what else can the parallelism apply but to the *equal and universal extent* of death and life?
>
> Verse 18: As through one man's offense condemnation came to *all men*, one man's righteous act resulted in justification of *all men*. Clearly here, condemnation and the justification of life are not being equally compared. It is the universal *extent* of Adam's

condemnation that is being compared with the universal extent of Christ's justification by the use of the word "all." That is the type. And note that Paul's use of "all" in this definitive verse identifies what he means by "many" in the other verses.

Verse 19: As one man's disobedience made many sinners—"the many" here, meaning all, for all have sinned and become disobedient—so one man's obedience will lead to "many" being made righteous—"the many" applying to all disobedient humankind. Again, since "disobedience" cannot be the parallel of "obedience," it is, therefore, the *extent* of the disobedience (which is total) that is being compared with the extent of "obedience"—which will be conferred upon all the disobedient and, therefore, also be total.

Verse 21: As sin reigns in death—and death is universal—so grace will reign in righteousness to eternal life—and that too will be universal, since the parallel is not between death and life, but between the universal extent of death and the universal effect of eternal life through Jesus Christ. Thus, it is not death that is a type of life, but rather the *extent* of death that is a type of the extent of life. That is the type.

So, do you see what's happening here? Paul is making it clear that the extent of the many who sinned is the same as the extent of the many who receive grace. (And, by the way, from the way that "many" is used as we have seen above, Paul is using the word in the way of "masses"—"the masses who sinned"—not in the sense of "most"—"most of those who sinned.") The extent of the many who died is equal to the extent of the many who receive life. He is focusing our minds on the parallel between what happened to all because of Adam, with what happened and will happen to all because of Christ—on the fact that the "all" who came under condemnation is the same as the "all" who are justified. The description of "the many" (the masses) is the same as the description of the "all" because the many (masses) who die as sinners are all of us and the many (masses) who finally are justified are also all of us.

Since the extent of the chaos Adam brought to the world is all-embracing—no one is unaffected—*Paul puts the results of Adam's life forward as the type of measurement by which to know the extent of the results of Christ's salvation.* Christ's salvation is also all-embracing—no one will finally be unaffected. *Adam's disaster, by nature and judgment, embraces the whole human race. Christ's redemption, by the gift of grace and restorative judgment, also embraces the whole human race.*

With Paul we have now reached the summit.

The Witness of the Gospel (2)

Pause.

Look out on the glorious view. From this vantage point, we can make out more clearly the other mountain peaks: Isaiah's "irrevocable oath" summit across the valley (see Isa 45:22–24), and that vast Ephesians range where all peoples are gathered together in one in Christ, everyone in heaven and on earth (see Eph 1:10). The whole majestic mountain range glows with glory. Sounds of praise to him who sits on the throne and to the Lamb (see Rev 5:8–14) echo through the peaks and canyons. How could Paul not have in mind such irrepressible, Old Testament declarations as these:

> O LORD, our Lord,
> how majestic is Your name in all the earth!
> (Ps 8:1 ESV)

> How awesome are your works!
> Through the greatness of Your power,
> Your enemies shall submit themselves to You.
> *All the earth shall worship You*
> *and sing praise to You;*
> They shall sing praises to Your name. Selah.
> (Ps 66:3–4)

> Among the gods there is none like You, O Lord;
> nor are there any works like your works.
> *All nations whom You have made*
> *Shall come and worship before You, O Lord,*
> *And shall glorify Your name.*
> For You are great and do wondrous things;
> You alone are God.
> (Ps 86:8–10)

> O You who hear prayer,
> *to You all flesh will come....*
> Oh God of our salvation,
> You who are the confidence of all the earth,
> And of the far-off seas.
> (Ps 65:2, 5)

So, now it's time to let the whole magnificent passage speak for itself:

> Therefore, just as through one man sin entered the world, and death through sin, and thus death spread to all men, because all sinned—(For until the law sin was in the world, but sin is not

imputed where there is no law. Nevertheless, death reigned from Adam to Moses, even over those who had not sinned according to the likeness of the transgression of Adam, who is a type of Him who was to come. But the free gift is not like the offense. For if by the one man's offense many died, much more the grace of God and the gift by the grace of the one Man, Jesus Christ, abounded to many. And the gift is not like that which came through the one who sinned. For the judgment which came from one offense resulted in condemnation, but the free gift which came from many offenses resulted in justification. For if by the one man's offense death reigned through the one, much more those who receive abundance of grace and of the gift of righteousness will reign in life through the One, Jesus Christ.) *Therefore, as through one man's offense judgment came to all men, resulting in condemnation, even so through one Man's righteous act the free gift came to all men, resulting in justification of life.* For as by one man's disobedience many were made sinners, so also by one Man's obedience many will be made righteous. Moreover the law entered that the offense might abound. But where sin abounded, grace abounded much more, so that as sin reigned in death, even so grace might reign through righteousness to eternal life through Jesus Christ our Lord. (Rom 5:12–21)

Objections: The "Many" and the "Few"

Nevertheless, sadly, there are those who object to this understanding of Paul's passage. They assert that Paul uses the word "many" in the sense of "a few" or "some." Not all will receive the grace, just the "many" (the few) who accept it. And not all will be obedient, just the "many" (the few) who repent and obey, the argument goes.

Let's do some reasoning here. Understand that reasoning is not out of place when it comes to interpreting Scripture. Certain Christians seem to have come to expect that biblical terminology is innately mystical, almost akin to magic. But those inspired men who wrote the Bible used rational thought processes to convey their message because people think rationally—well, they try to. The prophets weren't mystics. They didn't write in gibberish. They wrote propositionally, logically. And if we want to understand what the Holy Spirit inspired them to say, then we must try to follow their lines of thought.

The Witness of the Gospel (2)

(1) The interpretation above—that "many" and "all" have different meanings in this passage—can only be made by those who have isolated the words from their context. As we have already seen, it's clear from the text that "many" is not being used by Paul as "not all" or "a few," but as equivalent to "all" since he refers to "many" dying (v. 15), and obviously he means "all" because all die. And in reference to the many being made obedient, he's finishing off the type of "the many" who were made *disobedient*, and since in the first part of the type "the many" made disobedient means all mankind, because "all have sinned" (Rom 3:23), then the meaning of "many" in the second part of the type must also mean *all mankind*. Otherwise, the type doesn't match.

(2) But it's the wider context that shows us that this argument amounts to a mere quibble since Paul's whole reasoning is not to set the term "many" against the term "all," but to employ both terms to clinch his argument that in Adam the people who come under the far-reaching claws of sin and death are a type of the same people who come under the equally all-embracing arms of God's merciful grace in Christ.

(3) It's important to be aware that there's a price to pay in making "the many" to mean "the few." What we get for our money is *nonsense*. Because if we're going to interpret "many" as "few" in regard to those to whom grace abounds (v. 15) and yet at the same time, by the sheer force of reality, interpret "many" to mean "all" in regard to those who die (v. 15)—for all die—and if we're going to interpret "many" as "few" in regard to those who are made righteous (v. 19) and yet at the same time, by the sheer force of what stares us in the face, interpret "many" to mean "all" in regard to those who were made sinners (v. 19)—for all are sinners—*and*, in addition to that, if we're going to interpret "all" to mean "all" in regard to condemnation coming to all men but then interpret "all" to mean "few" in regard to those who will be justified, then we're engaging in gobbledygook, and we make Paul the author of it—his words, as slippery as eels. Further, if this argument were the correct one, then Paul, in spite of his learning and logic, would have utterly failed to carry through his analogy of Adam being a type of Christ. Better in that case to ignore the passage altogether. Which, of course, is what, for the most part, many believers do.

Many (not all!) complain that Paul's Romans Letter is "difficult." It is "difficult" only when its arguments for the salvation of all are ignored or resisted. When interpreters do not allow Paul the full logic and conclusions of his argument (because of their own biases towards a limited salvation), then Paul is "difficult," yes, because they simply cannot fit his reasoning for the salvation of all humanity into their own crimped, limited view of salvation. But when Paul is allowed his say, and his teaching of the salvation of all is let loose from its straitjacket, then Paul is not difficult at all. Everything locks into place.

Only Those Who "Receive"

Now for a final objection. Some contend that verse 17 implies that only *"those who receive the gift of righteousness* will reign in life with Christ." Reigning with Christ is limited to the few *who receive it*, while most of mankind will not, it's contended. Here's the verse:

> For if by the one man's offense death reigned through the one, much more those who receive abundance of grace and of the gift of righteousness will reign in life through the One, Jesus Christ. (Rom 5:17)

(4) Here's a classic case of isolating a verse from its surrounding meaning—its context, in other words. Naturally, if this were the only verse we had to go on, then it might appear the few who receive it will reign with Christ. But the connecting verses—the context—make this interpretation impossible.

(5) I've shown above how the verses in this passage are attempting to say the same thing in different ways. They cover the same ground, demonstrating that the type, the universal extent of Adam's fall, is fulfilled by the universal extent of Christ's redemption. So, it is inconsistent to pull out verse 17 and say, in effect, "Except this one—this one doesn't match the type."

(6) Furthermore, there's a little irony here because it's this verse that contains a unique detail demonstrating conclusively that all receive eternal life, not the few. In the verse, the people receiving "the abundance of grace" are spoken of as also receiving "the gift of righteousness" (v. 17). What is it to receive "the gift of righteousness"? It is to be justified, declared innocent, to be treated as if we had never sinned (see Rom 4:2–3). And who are justified? The few? No, the *all*. "Through one Man's righteous act the free gift came to *all men*, resulting in justification of life" (v. 18). Can you not hear God's unbreakable oath echoing in Paul's words: every tongue shall swear, "Surely *in the LORD I have righteousness* and strength" (Isa 45:23–24)?

(7) It's important to note, too, that "those who receive the abundance of grace" is a phrase that can be read as either a qualifying term or a

descriptive term. That is, it could read as "those, that is, the ones in particular who receive the grace" (qualifying) or "those, that is, all mankind, who, as a matter of fact (*de facto*), receive the abundance of grace" (descriptive). Since the near context of the whole passage states by various parallels that all mankind, which experiences Adam's sin, to that same extent also experiences Christ's righteousness, it must mean the latter (the descriptive). And, by the way, the original word here for "receive" is being used in the sense of the *recipients* of grace, rather than the people actively receiving. Young's Literal Translation of the Bible helps here by providing the literal rendering of the verse: "Much more those, who the abundance of the grace and of the free gift of the righteousness *are receiving*, in life shall reign through the one—Jesus Christ."

One more thing to be considered briefly:

(8) There is a more general, overarching context to this passage which indicates that Paul is referring to "all" mankind finally receiving justification and eternal life. And that is, *the comprehensive context of the whole Romans Letter itself.*

The Roman's Letter: The Unique Letter of "Alls"

- The loving wrath of God is upon *all*, both pagan and religious (Rom 1–3).
- *All* the world is under the power of sin (1–3).
- God gave the law so that *every* mouth (all) may be stopped (3:19).
- *All* the world is guilty before God (3:19).
- By the law *no* flesh (*none of all* humanity) will be justified in his sight (3:20).
- By the law is the knowledge of sin (to and upon *all*) (3:20).
- *All* are the same ("there is no difference") because *all* have sinned (3:23).
- *All* have fallen short of God's glory (3:23).
- Being (*all* being) justified freely by his grace (3:24).
- The promises of Abraham are that he will inherit "*the world*" (all) (4:13).

- Through Adam condemnation came to *all* (5:18).
- Through Christ justification and life come to *all* (5:18).
- *All* (the whole) creation is groaning with the birth pangs of redemption (8:22).
- *Nothing in all* creation will triumph over God's love (8:37–39).
- The *fullness* (all) of the nations (gentiles) will first come in (11:25).
- Then, *all* Israel will be saved (11:26).
- God has committed *all* to disobedience . . . (11:32).
- . . . that he might have mercy on *all* (11:32).
- Of him, through him, and to him are *all* things (11:36).

It is inconceivable that this letter of "alls," referring to God's all-embracing love and salvation for *all creation*, would have a parenthetical hole in the middle of it, stating, in effect, that only a few will be saved. Paul seriously meant what he said when he wrote, "Where sin abounded, grace abounded *much more*" (Rom 5:20).

Having taken in the vastness of salvation here at the summit of Paul's thoughts, give yourself time to take the glory of it in. Because the next thing we need to do is to look at *the process of thought that got Paul here*. What course did he map out to get to the summit? Fortunately, Paul, more than any other Bible writer, reveals the route he took. And it leads to the second great thing that God's loving propitiation of his wrath does for the world.

The Reasoning That Led to Paul's Conclusion

When Paul began his trek, he started out with a "therefore." "*Therefore*, just as through one man . . ." (Rom 5:12). That "therefore" means the whole discourse we've looked at was actually a *conclusion* to prior arguments that led him to that point. If the conclusion was the truth that Christ's redemption is going to be as far-reaching in its effect as Adam's sin is, then the arguments Paul assembled to bring his readers to that conclusion must be brimming with significance. And they are.

They bring us to another towering aspect of propitiation: *the revelation of the beloved sacrifice of Jesus Christ for the sin of the world and, by that, his gift of himself as love and righteousness for all humanity as the indispensable imperative for the salvation of everyone.*

The Witness of the Gospel (2)

Christ: The Righteousness for the World

We must go back to where Paul first stated that God's righteousness is revealed. He had spent the first few chapters of his letter talking about the corruption of all mankind, concluding that "there is none righteous, no not one" (Rom 3:10), but then, instead of the final judgment of God being pronounced upon the world as we might expect, he declares that "the righteousness of God is revealed" (3:21)—which is a final judgment of a different kind, a judgment to life instead of a judgment to death.

In referring to "righteousness," Paul's not talking here about that "glory of His majesty" when God "arises to shake the earth mightily" and everybody "cast[s] away his idols ... which they made, each for himself to worship, to the moles and bats, to go into the clefts of the rock ... from the terror of the LORD" (Isa 2:19–21). "The LORD alone will be exalted in that day" (v. 17), and it will be the time when the hearts of humanity will be melted to their core.

No, the righteousness that Paul speaks about here is a *gift*. It comes when we humans are at our lowest, when the whole world is "guilty before God" (Rom 3:19). This gift of righteousness is revealed to mankind, "apart from the law" (v. 21), which is Paul's way of saying "without any contribution of human effort"—when humans have nothing to offer God.

So, what is this righteousness?

It's not a question of what it is. It's a question of *who* it is.

> But now the righteousness of God apart from law is revealed ...
> even the righteousness of God, through faith in Jesus Christ, to all
> and on all who believe. (Rom 3:21–22)

Jesus is this righteousness. And the phrase "through faith in Jesus Christ" can be translated from the original language as "through *the faithfulness* of Jesus Christ," and that's most likely what Paul intends since it's in the next phrase that he mentions the faith of believers, and therefore it would not be necessary to mention it in this phrase. Young's Literal Translation reads, "And the righteousness of God is *through the faith of Jesus Christ* to all, and upon all those believing—for there is no difference." And the word for "faith" here is also translatable as "faithfulness." So, what we have in these words is God's awesome revelation of his Son—his dear Son's righteous faithfulness to his beloved Father from the cradle to the grave, a beautifully devoted and obedient life followed by obedience to an unjust and horrendous death for mankind.

The righteousness, then, is a *person*, not a quality. It is our Jesus, God's gift of his Son *to all and upon all who believe*.

But what is Paul meaning when he says the faithful righteousness of Jesus Christ is "to all and on all who believe"? What is the point he is making when he says "to all and on all"? (Note that this far-reaching phrase exactly lines up with his conclusion in chapter 5, that through *one* man's *righteous act*, the free gift came to all men, resulting in *justification* of life [see 5:18].)

It's to all and upon all precisely because "there is *no difference*" among mankind. All humanity is ruined. For "*all* have sinned, [*all*] fall short of the glory of God, *being justified*"—that is, all are being justified—"freely by His grace through the redemption that is in Christ Jesus" (Rom 3:22–24).

Well, this explains why humanity needs the righteous faithfulness of Christ, why it needs to be upon all (because all are in the same, equally tragic mess), but it still doesn't explain how it can possibly happen or how it could, by any stretch of the imagination, effectively reach the whole of the human race.

"Propitiation" and the Sacrifice of Christ

Then it is that Paul introduces that word "propitiation," which we explored in the last chapter. God set forth Jesus "as a propitiation by His blood, through faith" (Rom 3:25). *This is the door that opens the way for all the world's return*, by God's loving act of taking the world's judgment upon himself in his Son's death, and by giving the world Christ as their righteousness through his resurrection (see Rom 4:25). "He made Him who knew no sin to be sin for us, that we might become the righteousness of God in Him" (2 Cor 5:21).

Still, we are not yet given an understanding of the *process* by which Christ's righteous faithfulness is conferred upon mankind so that it can be said to be on "all and upon all." Is it infused into them by the Holy Spirit? Do they attain it through a disciplined life? Is it a result of their repentance?

If this righteousness has to be "infused," as many Christians believe, if it comes through a disciplined life, if it's to all and upon all as a result of their repentance so that they are now innately holy, if it comes to mankind by an internally generated faith—a faith that *we humans* produce in order to receive it (we'll be exploring faith in the next chapter)—then the salvation of all would be an impossibility, since it is inconceivable that all humanity would reach such a state, let alone the billions of people who came into the world and died throughout the millennia before Christ was born. And yet the answer is vital *if we are to follow the path Paul has carved out that brings us to the summit of his argument, that in Christ all men and women are justified.*

Righteousness "Accounted" to Humanity

And then—surprise—Paul reaches deep and far into the Old Testament, to the life of Abraham. This is a moment for an important side note. Many assume that Paul's ideas originate with him. And some take that so far as to accuse him of coming up with a gospel that is not found in the Bible. But this is a confusion between his *ideas* and his *way of expressing* them. Certainly, Paul is unique in the way he describes the ideas that are pressing in on his mind. But the truths themselves lie deep within the wells of Scripture. As we keep exploring the themes in volumes 1 and 2 of this book, we shall see that almost everything that Jesus reveals to Paul has its foundations in the Old Testament.

Hence the entrance of Abram in Paul's letter. God promised Abram a child, and through that child Abram would be "heir of the world" (Rom 4:13). The shock of this promise—even laughable (and "laughter," by the way, is the meaning of the name of Isaac, his son)—becomes evident when we realize that Abram (his name is commonly understood as "lord") was already an elderly man of seventy-five when he received the news. His wife, furthermore, was sixty-five and had never been able to bear children. And to top it off, when the child finally arrived, twenty-five years had passed since the promise had been given. Abram, now called Abraham, meaning "father of a multitude," had reached a hundred years and had felt himself as good as dead (Rom 4:19). Formerly barren Sarah was ninety.

But the important thing Paul wants to convey in this account is that as Abraham believed what God told him, "it was *accounted* to him as righteousness" (Rom 4:3). The word "accounted" is historic in its meaning for all. From the original language it can be translated "imputed" (as it is, in fact, translated in verse 6), "reckoned," "considered as," "attributed to," "charged to one's account." It's in this way that Paul, seeing Abraham as a type of the way God will treat all people, is introducing the process of how Christ's faithful righteousness comes "to all and upon all." In God's love he *counts* righteousness to mankind *as if it were theirs.* His compassion acts towards human beings as if they were righteous. Paul uses the same word in another of his letters, and it is translated mostly by the common expression, or some variation of it, "charge it to my account" (Phlm 1:18).

Only this line of thinking which Paul pursues meticulously could lead him to the conclusion that "justification of life" comes to all people (see Rom 5:18). God's propitiation involved God, by arrangement with his beloved Son, placing mankind's judgment upon Jesus, who was to stand in for humanity as a Son of Man on earth. Hence, Christ was a sacrifice on behalf of all humanity, standing *in the place of* all humanity, in a judgment on behalf of humanity, that the human race might be judged ("accounted") in his righteous humanity. "He [God] made Him who knew no sin *to be* sin for us, that we might become the righteousness of God in Him" (2 Cor 5:21). This is the astonishing, almost bizarre manner in which God's infinite compassion acts towards his lost creation.

A helpful way to think of it (though this is not included in Paul's letter) is the record of Abraham's near act of offering up his son, Isaac, on the altar some twelve years or so after his birth. Suddenly the angel stops him: "Don't lay a hand on the lad!" The knife held high, his arm freezes in place as he looks around and "there behind him was a ram caught in a thicket by its horns. So, Abraham went and took the ram and offered it up for a burnt offering *instead of his son*" (Gen 22:13). Just as the ram was sacrificed in the stead of Isaac, so the perfect life of Christ is offered up for us, a righteousness in the stead of our nonexistent righteousness. He was "delivered up because of our offenses and was raised because of our justification" (Rom 4:25).

It is the sacrificial life, death, and resurrection of Jesus as Son of Man on behalf of the human race he loves that is the argument, par excellence, for the salvation of all mankind.

Is Christ, Our Example, Enough?

But this meets with a silent sense of irrelevance by millions of Christians and humanists who see Christ's life as merely an example to live by. There's no doubt that Jesus is our example. But if that were the *only* meaning of Christ's life, it would never lead Paul to the conclusion that God would save us all since the unique example of Christ's life is so notoriously hard to exemplify. It's Paul's teaching in Romans that Christ's life is primarily *a loving sacrifice for humanity* that is leading Paul to the conclusion that God has made a way for the salvation of every human being, just as he had promised in his irrevocable oath.

You notice, when you read all the letters of Paul, how much emphasis he puts on the sacrificial death of Jesus because only the *beloved sacrificial death* stands in for all humanity. "Behold," says John, "the Lamb of God *who takes away the sin of the world!*" (John 1:29).

If Jesus were our example only, that fact, certainly, would be wonderful beyond words. Like dawn melting the night, Jesus' light rises upon us. The glory of the LORD in this one man (see Isa 60:1) preaching "good news to the poor," healing "the broken-hearted," and proclaiming liberty to the captives and "the opening of the prison to those who are bound" (Isa 61:1–2 ESV)! He's a meek and lowly man of such compassion, comforting, and consoling all who mourn (see v. 2). He encourages, giving them beauty in place of life's ashes, joy for mourning, praise for the spirit of heaviness (v. 3). Inner strength seems to flow from him as people, like bruised reeds, draw near to him, yet he doesn't snap them off as if they were useless (Isa 42:3). He's one whom many bow before, burned out like smoking flax, but he doesn't snuff them out (v. 3). He trims the spirit and makes it glow the brighter. He opens blind eyes. Thousands who sit in darkness he brings out of their prisons of sin and fear (v. 7). This is the beautiful, righteous humanity God intends for us all, and he brings it to the world in one man, Jesus, the Son of God, the Son of Man (Ps 45:2–4). How endlessly thankful we can be for that.

But if that is all he is for us, as wonderful as it is, it is not enough. Yes, Jesus Christ as our example *is not enough*. For if Jesus' life were an example only, if his life and death were a display of God's beauty only, the one who shed forth God's mercy to the few who were fortunate enough to cross his path for that brief moment of his existence on earth—if he were that and *only* that, it would fill those few with joy for a while; but then the anguish would fold around them after his light had left, and they'd feel the gloom again and realize time and again that they were not succeeding in their strenuous attempts to model themselves on such a pristine, unprecedented life and death. Then all those following afterwards, perceiving Jesus as no more than a teacher, a guru, proclaiming an impossible call to the world to follow him, would attempt to emulate Jesus' highly specialized philosophy of human development, delineated by him for our imitation. And the hope that every human being could become like him and be saved would gradually shift in shape, forming itself into an exasperating religious fantasy, a far-off dream that a few idealists would aspire to in their naiveté and yet, after a lifetime of self-sacrifice, find themselves as far from copying as the day they started out as spiritual rookies.

If this were all that Jesus is about, Paul would never have had the courage to posit the justification of all mankind because Jesus as *an example* hasn't a cat's whisker of being exemplified by all. And if that were all Jesus is for us, then Paul's statements of the *absoluteness*—the comprehensiveness—*of humanity's rescue by divine intervention would lead us to conclude that, at best, Paul was an idealistic dreamer, a man with a seriously bad habit of embellishing words with persistent exaggerations.*

Christ, a Unique Sacrifice

But Paul knew his Scripture, and now with the full revelation of Christ's crucifixion a few years earlier, he could see the meaning of the daily sacrifices of lambs on the altar that forever fixed in the minds of the ancient Israelites their need for something else—*someone else*—to substitute for their sins as they traveled with God through the drag of that wilderness journey (see Exod 29:38–44). Those lambs were a type of Christ, the Lamb of God, and his sacrifice for the sins of all the land. And now Paul saw with piercing, exhilarating clarity—now that Christ, the Messiah, had come—the meaning of those words written by Isaiah and then fulfilled some eight hundred years later in Paul's own lifetime:

> He was wounded for our transgressions,
> He was bruised for our iniquities;
> the chastisement for our peace was upon Him,
> and by His stripes we are healed. (Isa 53:5)

This understanding of Israel's mission to bring forth the sacrificial Messiah fills Paul's thoughts in his Romans Letter as he sees every blessing resting on humanity coming *through Jesus Christ*—through his substitutionary, sacrificial death and resurrected life. Look at the following examples:

- "God's righteousness *through the faithfulness of Jesus*" (Rom 3:22 ISV)
- Jesus "was delivered up *for* our offenses, and was raised *for* our justification" (4:25)
- We have "peace with God *through our Lord Jesus Christ*" (5:1)
- "*Through whom* also we have access by faith into this grace" (5:2)

- We are "reconciled to God *through the death of His Son*" (5:10)
- "We also rejoice in God *through our Lord Jesus Christ*" (5:11)
- Christ "*through whom* we have now received the reconciliation" (5:11)
- Grace reigns "to eternal life *through Jesus Christ our Lord*" (5:21)
- We are baptized "*into Christ Jesus,*" "*into His death*" (6:3)
- "We were buried *with Him* through baptism into death" (6:4)
- "Reckon yourselves to be . . . alive to God *in Christ Jesus our Lord*" (6:11)
- "You also have become dead to the law *through the body of Christ*" (7:4)
- "Who will deliver me . . . ? I thank God *through Jesus Christ*" (7:24-25)
- "There is therefore now no condemnation to those *who are in Christ Jesus*" (8:1)
- "We are children of God . . . heirs of God and joint heirs *with Christ*" (8:17)
- God shall "*with Him* [Jesus] also freely give us all things" (8:32)
- Nothing "shall be able to separate us from the love of God, *which is in Jesus*" (8:39)
- "To God, alone wise, be glory *through Jesus Christ*" (16:27)

The whole flavor of Paul's message in his Romans Letter is that the Creator and Father of mankind has decided to recover the human race through the work of a perfect substitute for humanity—Jesus Christ, Son of Man. He is the mediator between God and human beings since "a death has occurred that redeems them" from sin (Heb 9:15 ESV). Nothing is achieved without him, and everything he does as the Son of Man is *for and on behalf of human beings.* Christ has accomplished a victory for humankind that they hopelessly failed to accomplish. If God had decided to do his salvation work without a substitute, dealing with us human beings directly, given the shifting mental states and fickle emotions of human nature, he would never be able to accomplish his goal of saving all. But what he did for us in Christ was perfect and complete (Heb 9:14; 10:12, 14). "In Him all things [including us fallen, broken human beings] hold together" (Col 1:17 ESV) and "you are complete in Him" (Col 2:10). *The work of Christ in his lovely, complete, perfect, instead-of-us sacrifice—and by that very fact—secures the salvation of all human beings.*

It is the fact, then, of the propitiatory sacrifice alone that enables Paul to reach the mountain of his thoughts and arrive at the conclusion that *through this God-man's self-sacrificing, righteous act, the free gift came to all people* ("to all and on all"; Rom 3:22), resulting in "justification of life" (5:18). There is no other logical explanation for Paul's comparing the extent of Adam's sin equally with the extent of Christ's righteousness, and for using such absolute language as "one Man's righteous act" coming "to all" (Rom 5:18). Paul is a scholar. He shows care and thought in his writing. To sidestep his teaching on God's offering of Christ as a substitutionary, propitiatory sacrifice leaves us with the ultimately hopeless option that his language is over-the-top hyperbole, and that nothing he says can be taken with any seriousness.

But once his teaching of the propitiatory sacrifice is truly understood and accepted—a sacrifice embarrassing to the intellectual world of humanists and elite Christians who would far rather salvation be based on the qualities and accomplishments of individuals—then the sacrifice of Christ for the world, *ipso facto*, means the salvation of every human soul. It stands to reason, then, that the denial—or neglect—of the central truth of Christ's sacrificial death for humanity is the primary reason that the Christian church cannot fathom the salvation of *all* God's creation.

Paul Almost at the Summit

And now comes Paul's semi-conclusion. It's his narrow lead-up to the summit. What he is about to say could be a breathtaking summit in itself, if we didn't already know that just beyond the next rise is the ultimate height.

> For when we were still without strength, in due time Christ died for the ungodly. For scarcely for a righteous man will one die; yet perhaps for a good man someone would even dare to die. But God demonstrates His own love toward us, in that while we were still sinners, Christ died for us. Much more then, having now been justified by His blood, we shall be saved from wrath through Him. For if when we were enemies we were reconciled to God through the death of His Son, much more, having been reconciled, we shall be saved by His life. And not only that, but we also rejoice in God through our Lord Jesus Christ, through whom we have now received the reconciliation. (Rom 5:6–11)

The Witness of the Gospel (2)

The first thing to note in Paul's statement here is what we have established in the last few pages. Christ died *for* people—for people without strength, for the ungodly, for sinners, for enemies. *For them—on behalf of them.* Nothing could be clearer than this. Christ's death was an *in-place-of* death, a *substitutionary* death. This fact alone leads Paul to his summit conclusion that Christ's "righteous act" results in "justification of life" for all (Rom 5:18).

The second thing to note in this passage is that Christ died *for people who reached the depths of their inability to respond to him. People "without strength," people who are "ungodly," people who are "sinners," people who are even "enemies."* Paul's deepest, personal awareness of this would have come from his own experience, an enemy of Jesus, as he was before his conversion, arresting Christians, carting them off to jail in the early hours, and even overseeing their execution in some cases (see Acts 7:58; 8:1; 9:1–2, 13–14; 22:4–5; 26:9–11; Gal 1:13; 1 Tim 1:13).

This "blasphemer," this "persecutor," this "insolent man" (yes, Paul!) Jesus swiveled around on a dime to become the greatest Christian missionary the world has ever seen. He must have heard, too, through Peter, how Jesus turned each searing thrust of pain into a prayerful cry for his enemies as they were pounding the nails into his hands: "Father, forgive them, for they don't know what they are doing" (Luke 23:34 NLT). And the words of the Son of Man, that he came "to seek and to save the lost [perished]" (Luke 19:10 ESV), would be etched on Paul's mind. Unquestionably, Paul would be fully aware of that awesome prophecy in Isaiah regarding the Messiah—a description of the meaning of Christ's death that is not matched even in the New Testament: "The chastisement for our peace was upon Him, and by His stripes we are healed. All we like sheep have gone astray; we have turned, everyone, to his own way; and the LORD has laid on Him the iniquity of us all" (Isa 53:5–6).

God's gift of his Son to the world is, therefore, the gift of his Son *to the world*. Not to the few who might have the spiritual wherewithal to follow his example. But to the world who do not even have the wit or the opportunity to know who he is. Who are wandering around like hapless, dithering sheep. Whose minds are like a severed limb that cannot find the necessary rhythm to walk in his ways. Whose arms have grown too weak for want of the nourishment of human affection to hold on to the embrace of God. Whose hearts are dried like leather for searching for the water of life in the wrong places—in broken wells that hold no water (Jer 2:13).

The third thing to note about this passage is the *universal* nature of those whom Christ died for. Who in the world is not a sinner? Who in the world is not without strength? Who in the world is not ungodly? Who in the world is not *innately* an enemy of God at heart? Paul here is talking about *all mankind*.

And the fourth thing to note about this passage is the most stunning fact of all, one that causes our minds to writhe and twist at the apparent contradiction of ideas.

Reconciled While Enemies

Christ's death for weak, ungodly sinners who are at odds with God by the very fact of their enemy-state is *a reconciliation*. Notice that verses 6, 8, and 10 of this chapter are parallel thoughts—a style that Paul uses when comparing the two Adams a little later. In layout it looks like this:

5:6—*When we were without strength and ungodly* . . . Christ died for us.

5:8—*When we were still sinners* . . . Christ died for us.

5:10—*When we were enemies* . . . we were reconciled . . . through the death of his Son.

So, then, "Christ's death" in verses 6 and 8 equates with God's reconciliation of humans through that death in verse 10. Verse 10 states that while humans were enemies they were "reconciled to God through the death of his Son." Paul's paralleling of his thoughts here shows that *Christ's death is more than something tentative. Christ's death is an actual reconciliation.* It is God, through his loving act of placing the world's judgment upon his Son, who is bringing that world back to himself.

The Error of Christ's Death Being Only a Potential

But—forgive me if I'm wrong—my sense is that you are not getting what I just wrote. You are most likely reading it as "Christ died for sinners *if they accept it*." If they believe it. If they repent. You may not be aware yet how profoundly this kind of thinking blocks Christians from believing that God will save all humanity.

Where did the idea that Christ died for sinners if they accept it come from? Certainly not from some meaning buried in Paul's original text. *It has gained traction in our minds from long centuries of mental conditioning that persistently posits salvation as something that, in the ultimate, humans bring about by their own "decision-making."* And since Paul's teaching as it stands simply does not fit that permutation, we have unconsciously added a concept to it to force the fit.

This thinking, that Christ died for sinners if they accept it, turns Jesus' sacrificial death into a potential only. It is operative—effective—only to the extent that human beings believe it. *Christ's sacrifice consequently becomes limited by the will of his creation*, who condescend either to accept it or to reject it. For hundreds of millions of Christians this is a colossal sticking point, preventing their belief in the salvation of all mankind.

The issue of humanity's failure to accept Christ's sacrifice is thus conceived as being the shoreline where the waters of salvation for all the world meet resistance and ebb tragically away. Acceptance—rather, the absence of it—is presumed to be the barrier that halts salvation in its tracks, for if mankind does not accept God's loving work in Christ for them—and the majority do not—then doesn't that spell doom for the majority of humankind, and the salvation of all a mere fantasy?

There's hardly a preacher or teacher in the land, nor a Bible scholar or commentator, who will tell you that Christ's death for the ungodly is an *actual reconciliation*. What most teachers and preachers will pronounce is that Christ's death for ungodly, helpless sinners and enemies of Christ is real only *provisionally*. That is, its benefits are proffered but can be withdrawn, depending on humanity's embrace of it. Though Christ's death for sinners actually took place, its effectiveness is only a potential, it is said, until you, who sit in the pew, come forward and say yes to it. Hence, the majority of Christians unconsciously read Paul's words regarding Christ's death for sinners in the following way:

> For when we were still without strength, in due time Christ died for the ungodly *potentially*.

This kind of understanding of Christ's death for the ungodly could not possibly have led Paul to his Himalayan thoughts that through one man's righteous act, justification of life came to all men (Rom 5:18). And it is clearly not what Paul says. His statement is,

> When we were enemies we were reconciled to God through the death of His Son. (Rom 5:10)

Period.

Is Paul unaware of subtlety, of nuance? Of the variations of color in the way to express things? He certainly shows subtlety in his appeal to Philemon regarding his slave, and his persuasive charm in his second letter to the Corinthians. So, couldn't he have added a little nuance here—"When we were enemies, *we who accepted him* were reconciled to him through the death of his Son"—if that is what he meant?

No, he clearly could not because that's not what he meant. The whole context of his statement is "propitiation"—God's compassionate act of taking the judgment for mankind upon himself through his precious Son (John 12:31–32). By that sacrificial death all humanity *in its enemy-state is reconciled*, so that "much more, having been reconciled, *we shall be saved* by His life" (Rom 5:10). It is that glorious reconciliation that God brings about in himself through his Son which sets in motion all the heavenly forces of grace to complete the process of gathering together "in one all things in Christ, both which are in heaven and which are on earth in Him" (Eph 1:10).

Furthermore, Paul could not have meant "when we were enemies, *we who accepted him* were reconciled to him through the death of his Son" because that reasoning would not have led him to the conclusion at the summit that "through one Man's righteous act the free gift came to *all* men, resulting in justification of life" (Rom 5:18).

That it is enemies who are reconciled—these are the final few steps Paul makes in his argument before leaping across the crevasse into his great presentation of the two Adams at the summit. Now, the mountaintop vista makes it clear that the people whom Christ, the second Adam, justifies are precisely those helpless, ungodly, sinful enemies—humanity itself. They are reconciled by the supreme sacrifice God made in his Son. It is big thoughts like these that have led Paul to the biggest summit of all, that the grace of Christ abounds to *all* mankind.

The End of an Enigma

We are forced, therefore, by the reasoning of faith to say that if the effectiveness of Christ's death is no more than a *latent* power that will spring to life only if mankind is willing to accept it, then Paul's arguments are shorn of meaning, and he remains the enigma that hundreds of books about him have tried and failed to solve over the centuries, for there would be no way to explain why he uses such definitive, absolute language to describe something so supposedly tentative and limited. And if Christ's death is merely latent, suspended in tension until and if mankind accepts it, then, in the light of humanity's variableness, there is categorically no chance that all mankind could be rescued. If Christ's sacrificial death stands as a *potential* only—*a tentative, provisional arrangement* until and if mankind deigns to receive it, in which case it only then becomes effective reality—then no matter how much God declares an oath that every knee will ultimately bow, his oath is made impotent and ludicrous by the sheer arrogance of most of humanity's will to trump that oath by their rejection of it. Shall our idolatry towards the supremacy of the human will triumph over the unbreakable oath of Almighty God? In the end, shall the just God and Savior himself, before whom all men are as grasshoppers (Isa 40:22), bow before the will of the world?

When God made his oath—which this scholar of a man, Paul, embraced fully (see Rom 14:10–11; Phil 2:9–11)—God revealed a self-knowledge that most humans do not have of him. He knows the persuasive power of his sacrificial love. He knows the compelling revelation of his judgments when all is brought to light. He knows the weakest points of people's stubbornness, and the strongest yearnings of their beings. He has the power to persuade the heart, not to force it by reducing humans to automatons, but to reverse the course of its flow by the overwhelming grip of ultimate reality, which altogether shocks, turns, and draws humanity. God is able to "incline our hearts to Himself" (1 Kgs 8:58).

Asking the Right Question About Faith

Where then, does a person's decision to believe come in? What is the role of faith? Isn't it a determining factor? By this point, some of my readers may be screaming these questions at me at the frantic turn of every page. I don't hesitate for a second to say faith is *paramount*. "Believe on the Lord Jesus Christ and you will be saved" (Acts 16:31). There can be no salvation without faith. But ask the wrong question and you'll get the wrong answer.

The question is not "Is faith necessary?" Rather, "How does faith come?" And, "Where does it come from?" Only a proper answer to these questions can lead to an understanding of the victory of God's irrevocable, unbreakable oath to the world. Only a proper answer shows how the vibrancy of the gospel makes sure God's oath comes to its fulfillment. Only a proper answer will give us that magnificent view from the summit where we finally come to see that the God of all the earth will "inherit all nations" (Ps 82:8).

So then, is faith in Christ a product of the human mind, or does it come from the mind of God?

Chapter 4

The Witness of Faith (1)
Faith–A Human Thing? Or a God Thing?

FAITH—THAT HEAVENLY INTRIGUE. THAT open secret of how God rescues all mankind.

But not according to some. There's a view adrift in perhaps most places in the Christian world that faith is a decision of a person's will—a response to God coming from humanity's side—our part of the bargain while God fulfills his. And hence, faith is far from a radical miracle that God plants in the heart—far from that "open secret" that God possesses in his arsenal of grace to rescue all mankind from its trap. Faith's just a human-powered thing by which a person accepts Christ and is consequently saved.

So, it's no surprise, following this line of thought, that you'd end up concluding that the final outcome of humanity's salvation is in the hands of human beings, not in the hands of God, since God respects a person's free will and allows them to reject Christ if they wish. And since most of unconverted humanity will do just that, then the majority of the world will be lost eternally by their own choice. *Voila!* The "heavenly intrigue" of faith has gone up in smoke. Human beings are back in the driver's seat, getting on with their eternal destiny—or not bothering with it at all.

Apart from its paralyzing lack of drama, the view that faith is an issue of a person's free-will choice is entirely false and devastates the good news of the gospel, as I will show in this chapter and the next. What it does explain, certainly, is why so much modern Christianity is soulless and dull—incapable of perceiving the good mind of God for the saving of all mankind.

Another understanding of faith—one which we will now begin to explore from Scripture—is that faith is a gift of God's passionate love to the world. It is an ingredient of the good news itself, and, as we shall see, God moves heaven and earth to implant it in the human heart, whether here on earth or in the throes of the final judgment. We shall discover in the next two chapters that only a life moved upon by God through what he has done for humanity in Christ is capable of believing. The drama of the gospel, in part, is God's skillful way of positioning human beings to receive it.

Based on this view of faith, and keeping in mind God's irrevocable oath, the biblical evidence in the ensuing pages leads us to the following conclusion: *The final outcome of humanity's salvation is the result of God's triumphant grace, not the result of mankind's choice of faith.* Through the sacrifice of God's Son, *God has the power to persuade people's hearts and renew their wills, and therefore he is able to gift them with faith.* Since, as we have seen, every tongue will swear allegiance to God, that allegiance will come from an act of faith in God who will have formed that faith in them, and therefore all will be saved eternally because God so loves the world (see John 3:16) and is victor over it (Col 2:15).

But before we explore the kind of faith the gospel speaks of, we need to consider why the issue matters in the first place. Do we really care where faith comes from as long as we have it?

Why It Matters Where Faith Comes From

It matters because the world is in a continual state of sin and suffering. That little boy in Yemen who falls on his daddy, begging him to wake up after he is killed by a bomb at a wedding party? A month later he still sat in prolonged silence except to be heard occasionally repeating dread words about the day his father wouldn't wake up. What will become of that little boy in the large scheme of things? He's surrounded by a Muslim culture unlikely to be influenced by the message of the gospel. He'll be raised a Muslim, and his perception of life will be scarred by the loss of his beloved *abba*. How will he—and millions more like him—come up with faith in Christ?

It matters because of that little girl who was gang-raped, killed, and thrown off the bus—and because of other abused girls and boys, countless as the sands of the sea throughout the ages.

It matters because of those millions abandoned by the Nazis in the gas chambers who fought for their last breath, their minds with no space left for faith, so chock-full of terror they were.

It matters because of the ten million or more children living by their wits on the streets and under bridges in India. How do they believe in one they have never known? How can faith arise in them, whose little fingers can barely reach the master's table—if only they had a master, or a table?

It matters because of the hundreds of millions who have withered away in the harrowing silence of famine, and the countless numbers lost to disease, and the myriads sold into ancient and modern slavery, and those victims of that twisted trinity of tyrants, Stalin, Mao, and Hitler, sadists to the core, who destroyed more people than all those who died in the hundreds of wars prior to that time over the last two thousand years put together, thus marking down the twentieth century as the most violent in history.

It matters because heaps upon heaps of humanity suffer from maltreatment of all kinds, physical, emotional, sexual, religious maltreatment, like the young woman who today is trying to scrape up some sort of meaning to life because as a child she was passed from father to uncle and back again for sexual favors, her mother, unable to defend her, dead from alcohol poisoning.

It matters because if you are an "average" human being, you were probably born in the "wrong" hemisphere—the majority of the world's masses, that is—which was not exposed, mostly, to Christian evangelism. Places where the majority of the world lives—like China, Japan, India, Pakistan, Malaysia, Indonesia, Borneo, and other almost nameless places on the globe, the tone of whose pagan cultures drowns out any sweet strains of Jesus that might pass their way. How can they believe? And then again, being born in the "right" hemisphere, Europe, North and South America, and Australia by culture, is not that much of an advantage in view of the post-Christian culture of the West and our seemingly endless capacity to abuse ourselves. Who, even in our lands, can create faith in Christ out of their ashes?

So, it matters because all human beings are under the power of sin and death, damaged goods from the start. Emotionally tainted the moment we arrive on this disordered planet, our already innately sin-scarred self, along with childhood wounds piled on top, form views of life and God that later get set in mental concrete. Can humans possibly initiate faith from a nature such as this? It's not simply a matter of behavior we're talking about. The evil that spawns our unbelief and sins emerges from the depths of our soul, and at a time when we didn't even know we had a soul, at a time when we couldn't possibly understand where our impulses came from and where they would ultimately end up. Humans are in bondage to incomprehensibly dark forces. Who can possibly deny that if faith in the generosity of God, our Redeemer, is to stir in the human heart, it has to come from above—from God's side—not from below, where humanity permanently wallows in its delusions and darkness?

False Origins of Faith Result in a Distorted Gospel

It's this wider consideration of the world, this more comprehensive view of humanity's true horrors, that forces us—by the glaring fact of the world's devastating afflictions—to an urgent reexamination of Scripture for fresh understanding of how faith in the Creator-Redeemer reaches the hearts of *all* his creation. Spiritual darkness is so widespread throughout the world that to expect humanity to produce universal belief in God and his Savior, Jesus Christ, is simply unimaginable.

It's no wonder Christians have difficulty comprehending God's plan to save everyone when their assumptions of faith presuppose that it is a matter of the will to choose to believe. The result of this human-centered understanding of faith spawns that pathetic myth that most of humanity will be lost because they don't know Christ, or conversely, they will be saved because they don't know any better!

Such shoddy reasoning leaves a world without hope and Christians in the embarrassing position of holding a Bible in their hand that has not been properly explored. Inevitably, they sidle up to the unspoken belief that it is only the super-few who will be saved by faith in Christ because they supposedly possess by fortune and upbringing some quality ingredient that enables them to believe, and which the rest lack—especially if they're born in the wrong place.

No amount of protestation from those Christians who insist they do not hold this view will cut the mustard. No matter what your creed says, if you drive faith to the edge of the precipice insisting that the reason God will not save all the world is that the majority of mankind simply thrills to the rush of plunging headlong over the cliff into unbelief, and if they would just stop their folly and use a bungee cord of will to bring their faith to safe ground, God would save them, then you have turned faith into a condition of salvation that humans must provide; and faith, instead of being an action of God's grace, becomes a work of the will's presumed flexibility by which humans spring back from the abyss onto the sturdy platform of salvation. The outcome of the world's salvation is thus in the hands of humanity, not in the hands of God. Try as you might with the most sophisticated theological arguments, there is no getting around this.

But then, once again, the gospel speaks into human darkness. As its cadences vibrate in your ear you pick up a different melody of faith from the jarring tones that so much Christian teaching prattles on about.

Faith, the Link Let Down from the Kingdom of Heaven

As we saw earlier, the Romans Letter demarcates the dividing line of history. On that demarcation line stands the lone figure of the Son of Man, Jesus Christ, God's gift to all the world. Before the cross is the history of mankind under the reign of sin and death. After the cross is mankind's history under the reign of the righteous life in Christ.

But this "before and after" demarcation is not one of historical time, but of *spheres of existence*. Without the sacrificial death of Christ and his resurrection, humanity knows only a one-world existence, the universal devastation of life under Adam. In Christ's atoning sacrifice and resurrection, the world can know—and will know—the universal liberation into justification and life. *It is through this reign of the one man, Jesus Christ, that faith arises.*

A careful study of the Romans Letter makes it clear that faith is not a link that originates in Adam's kingdom of sin and death, which then latches on to the kingdom of Christ. Rather, faith is *the link let down from the kingdom of Christ itself*, which hauls us out of that dark kingdom of Adam into the light of Christ's kingdom.

The evidence for this heavenly origin of faith is made clear by the way Paul, in his Romans Letter, describes the *arrival of faith*—how it comes to be in the hearts of men and women.

We've examined together some of the following verses in the light of God's righteousness that he provides through his Son to all the world. Now we'll look at these verses and others from the viewpoint of faith.

> But now, apart from the Law, God's righteousness is revealed
> . . . —God's righteousness through the faithfulness of Jesus, the

Messiah—for all who believe. For there is no distinction among people. (Rom 3:21–22 ISV)

After all mankind's pagan and religious (Rom 1–3) efforts at righteousness, mankind remains thrashing about in its own catastrophic disorder. Then God's righteousness is revealed without any contribution from mankind ("without the law"), but through the faithfulness of Jesus Christ to all believers (Rom 3:22 ISV).

The intrigue of faith begins right here.

The verse could be saying that the revelation of God's righteousness is *the unveiling of his Son*, made known to us by faith. That is, that God's righteousness is not only a revelation of God's Son but also the *faith-knowledge to know who he is*. In other words, that faith is *an aspect of the righteousness* that he reveals so that when God gives his righteousness to us in his Son, he also gives us the gift of faith to *understand and believe it*. Can this be what Paul is saying, rather than the traditional understanding that God's righteousness is revealed and mankind, by its self-generated act, responds to it and accepts it by faith? The verse itself doesn't provide us with a definite answer, but the possibility is tantalizing. We need more to go on.

And we have.

Justification and Faith, Both Acts of Grace

First, Paul proceeds to explain that God's righteousness in Christ *justifies* a person—in other words, God's righteousness in Christ is what declares the sinner, or treats him, as innocent, as righteous:

> The righteousness of God . . . is revealed . . . for there is no difference, for all have sinned . . . being justified freely by His grace through the redemption that is in Christ Jesus. (Rom 3:21–24)

So, by grace a person is justified—that is, declared innocent and righteous by the graceful redemption that comes through the work of Jesus Christ. Clearly, then, justification is *God's act*. It is God who justifies a person by his free grace.

Yet, intriguingly, Paul goes on to say something else: "Therefore we conclude that a man is justified *by faith* apart from the deeds of the law" (Rom 3:28).

Now, he just said a few verses earlier that a person is justified by *grace*—God's act—through the redemption that is in Christ. But now he says that someone is justified by *faith*. So, which is it? What are we to make of this? Is Paul confused? Has he forgotten what he'd said previously so that he fails to follow through with a consistent thought? It's no good saying that we are justified by grace and that faith is simply the way we receive that justification, because Paul said we are justified by grace *and* we are justified by faith. The only possible explanation for this seeming contradiction is that *faith is part of God's grace*. If we are declared innocent (justified) by God's act of grace in Christ and it is also said that we are declared innocent by faith, then the faith by which a person is declared innocent (justified) must also be part of God's act of grace in Christ by which he is justified.

Faith Comes to a Person "Without the Law"

Paul continues further to say that sinners are "justified by His blood" (Rom 5:9). And he later says that "it is *God* who justifies" (Rom 8:33 ESV). It's the atoning work of Christ on the cross (his blood) and God himself who justifies a person, accounting them righteous. So it cannot be that faith *as an act of the human heart* justifies, otherwise it is not God only but the person, finally, who justifies themselves. Unless we are going to admit to confused thinking here on Paul's part, we must positively affirm that if a person is justified by the initiative of God through Christ's death (his blood), then for Scripture to speak of that person as being justified by faith means that their faith is also a part of God's initiative.

Furthermore, notice that Paul says righteousness comes to a person without the law (without any human contribution). But he also *says the same about faith*:

> Therefore, we conclude that a man is justified by faith *apart from the deeds of the law*. (Rom 3:28)

Just as God's righteousness comes to humans from God's side—without the works of the law, that is—so also faith comes to humans from God's side, without the works of the law.

With relentless precision, Paul drives home the origin of humanity's justification to life and the faith that makes it known to them. So now he turns to Abraham for further evidence of how grace and faith come. What shall we say of Abraham, Paul asks.

The Evidence of Abraham

> Abraham believed God, and it was accounted to him for righteousness. (Rom 4:3)

What does Paul conclude from this passage, which he quotes from the book of Genesis? He notes that if Abraham's faith had been "a work"—something produced from his own mind—it would not have been *accounted* to him—imputed, treated as if it were his. It would have been acknowledged as a work that he owned and produced. In fact, in a certain sense God would have been in Abraham's "debt" for a work well done (see Rom 4:4). But since faith was accounted to him, it could not have originated from Abraham but from God as an act of grace. And this is reinforced by the fact that his faith was accounted as *righteousness*. As the gospel consistently shows, righteousness comes from God alone. No human is righteous, "no, not one" (Rom 3:10). *When God accounts Abraham's faith as righteousness it is clear that that faith is a righteousness from God's side, not from the human side.*

Abraham was a member of the fallen race of Adam, like all of us. That race is described as being under the power of sin and death (see Rom 3:9; 5:12). Abraham happened to be an honorable pagan, a courageous man, a leader of men and women, a brilliant strategist, an outstanding financier, a great organizer, fair and just to a household of probably some five hundred souls. So, he might have had something to boast about—*but not before God* (Rom 4:2) because he stood on the wrong side of history, a member of fallen, corrupt humanity. None of his moral and ethical standing bore any weight as righteousness before God. That's why faith was *accounted as righteousness to him*, because *it did not come from him*. It came as a gift of God's righteousness to him, accounted to him as if it were his.

So significant is this truth about the divine origin of faith that Paul speaks of faith being accredited (imputed, accounted) to humans (Rom 4:5) and righteousness being accredited to humans *in the same breath* (Rom 4:6).

Certainly, righteousness comes from *outside* of human beings since, by necessity, it has to be accounted to them because all are under sin—they have no righteousness of their own (Rom 3:9). So, then, faith must also come from outside of them since it also is accounted or credited to them—they have no faith of their own.

The Significance of the Term "The Righteousness of Faith"

Thus, in magnificent climax, Paul brings to the stage the astonishing expression *"the righteousness of faith"* (Rom 4:11, 13). It would be unthinkable for him to use such phraseology if he believed that faith emanated from humans—not, surely, after building the case throughout his whole letter that all mankind is under sin (Rom 3:9) and cannot, therefore, produce righteousness (Rom 3:19–21).

When Paul uses the phrase "the righteousness of faith," he is playing it as a counterpoise to the Jewish argument of "the righteousness of the law." But it is not the counterpoise of "You get *your* righteousness from the *law*. But I get *mine* through *faith*."

No, it is the counterpoise of "You get your righteousness from the law, but I have no righteousness, and I have to rely on the righteousness of another." You get your goodness from yourself—from what you believe is your natural capacity to be obedient to God. But for me? *For me, "the righteousness of faith" means the righteousness of Christ for me, in whom I have faith*. Faith in Christ is that faith-realization that I am crushed and killed by the law—that is, by all human attempts to be good (see Gal 2:19–20). I no longer believe that I can generate righteousness. The revelation of my sin and brokenness and the revelation of Christ who died for me have made it clear to me that it is only as God acts mercifully towards me, *as if I were a righteous person*, that I know that God alone is my Righteousness. By this I am both crushed and made alive.

The Alien Nature of Faith in Christ

Thus, this is a faith so *unnatural* to human instinct, so alien to our thoughts, so contrary to our concepts of morality, so annoying to our spirit, so beyond our natural resources, that it cannot possibly flow from the energies of the human being—and certainly not from the confidence of their heart. *Faith in Christ is a human absurdity*. It is a faith that destroys human confidence, brings us to humility, and leads to confidence in God only. *The very content of this faith is juxtaposed to human nature—counterintuitive to it—indicating that it has to be a grace from God because a human being cannot produce it*. It is faith from God's side, not humanity's side. It is the righteousness of faith and therefore comes from the righteous love of Christ.

You notice how this makes much more sense of Paul's question, "Where is boasting then?" He answers it himself by saying that it is excluded by the law (the principle) of faith (see Rom 3:27). The thought behind this is that we can't boast about faith because it originates from God, not human nature. Whenever human beings get a little conceited about the fact that we believe and others don't, they've fallen for the delusion that faith is something *they've* produced.

Furthermore, consider, later on, how Paul has the unflinching boldness to say that we sinners were *reconciled* to God *"while we were enemies."* To be reconciled to God is to be justified and accounted righteous (compare Rom 5:9 with Rom 5:10). How can this be? An enemy is in darkness. They have "together become unprofitable" (Rom 3:12). It is impossible, therefore, to conceive that the righteousness of faith could emanate from a person while they are an enemy. The only way an enemy is reconciled while they are still an enemy is that the light of faith—faith in Christ—comes to them from God while they are still in their pitch-black gloom. It could not come from their darkened soul. Light penetrates darkness. Darkness does not penetrate light.

Jesus' Witness to the Origins of Faith

And let it not be said that this is solely Paul's teaching. Jesus turns things upside down with words that run our spiritual paradigms into the ground. We tend to think that we "came to Jesus" at such and such a time and place in our lives, that we "gave our hearts to Jesus," "came forward and made a commitment to the cross," and similar expressions. But what about these mind-bending words from the lips of Jesus himself:

> *All that the Father gives Me will come to Me,* and the one who comes to Me I will by no means cast out. (John 6:37)

> *You did not choose Me, but I chose you,* and appointed you that you should go and bear fruit. (John 15:16)

> You have given Him authority over all flesh, *that He should give eternal life to as many as You have given Him.* (John 17:2)

> I have manifested your Name *to the men whom You have given me* out of the world. They were Yours, You gave them to Me. (John 17:6)

The Witness of Faith (1)

> This is the will of the Father who sent Me, that *of all He has given Me* I should lose nothing, but should raise it up at the last day. (John 6:39)

In the light of these words from Jesus, it's necessary to start seeing the engine at the front of the train instead the back. From what Jesus is saying here, isn't it a fact that when a person "gives their heart to Jesus," they're responding rather than initiating? They're not the one in the driver's seat. There's something else going on. Some mysterious force that seizes a person's heart and draws them into the light. That mysterious force is, of course, the exuberant love of God through the Holy Spirit, drawing someone on in Christ. Jesus is saying, in effect, our coming to him is not an act of faith coming from our side. It is a gift of faith coming from God's side, moving us forward in Christ.

> No one can come to Me *unless the Father* who sent Me *draws him*; and I will raise him up at the last day. (John 6:44)

> No one can come to Me *unless it has been granted* to him by My Father. (John 6:65)

What other explanation can there be for Jesus' words than that "giving our hearts to Jesus" is an act initiated by God, not by us humans?

And what, furthermore, of Peter's statement of faith when he declared to Jesus, "You are the Christ, the Son of the living God"? Did this faith in who Jesus is come from Peter's side, generated by him?

> Jesus answered and said to him, "Blessed are you, Simon Bar-Jonah, *for flesh and blood has not revealed this to you, but My Father who is in heaven*." (Matt 16:16–17)

Here it's clearly stated that flesh and blood—that is, natural, fallen humanity—does not come up with belief in who Jesus is. Peter could not have believed that Jesus is God's Son unless it had been "revealed to him" by God. *Faith in Christ is, therefore, as much a process of revelation as the revelation about Christ itself is.* "A man can receive nothing," Jesus said, "unless it has been given to him from heaven" (John 3:27).

Faith Is *Conferred*

And then there's the evidence from Paul's other letters. In his first letter to Timothy, Paul reminisces with his young protégé (not so young, actually; Timothy was about thirty-five, and Paul, perhaps in his early sixties):

> And the grace of our Lord came to me in overflowing fulness, *conferring faith on me* and the love which is in Christ Jesus. (1 Tim 1:14 WEY)

The words in the original language suggest that grace overflowed super-abundantly on Paul *in company with and along with* faith. Other translations of this verse are equally enlightening:

> The grace of our Lord was poured out on me abundantly, *along with the faith* and love that are in Christ Jesus. (NIV)

> *The grace of our Lord overflowed for me with the faith and love* that are in Christ Jesus. (ESV)

> The grace of our Lord was more than abundant, *with the faith and love which are found in Christ Jesus*. (NASB)

And so, Paul—this man with the blood-surge of love for God—ascribed the whole process of salvation to God. This Old Testament scholar knew his Scriptures. He knew that "the way of a man is not in himself; it is not in man who walks to direct his steps" (Jer 10:23). It was God who had "also done all our works in us" (Isa 26:12). He knew that "a man's steps are of the LORD" (Prov 20:24). He knew that "the king's heart is in the hand of the LORD, like the rivers of water; He turns it wherever He wishes" (Prov 21:1). And that's why, in the marked humility of this man who described himself as the chief of sinners (1 Tim 1:15), he could say,

> For by grace you have been saved through faith, and that not of yourselves; it is the gift of God, not of works, lest anyone should boast. . . . For we are His workmanship. (Eph 2:8, 10)

If faith were of human origin, we could have no confidence at all that the whole world will be saved because if there is one consistency about us humans, it is our *unfaithfulness*. But if faith is of God, then we can have all the confidence in the world that all humanity will be rescued because *God is faithful to himself and to his unbreakable oath* that at the Name of Jesus every knee will bow, of those in heaven, and of those on earth, and of those under the earth, and that every tongue will confess that Jesus Christ is Lord, to the glory of God the Father. (Phil 2:10–11 NASB)

I have sworn by Myself;
The word has gone out of My mouth in righteousness,
And shall not return,
That to Me every knee shall bow,
Every tongue shall take an oath.
He shall say,
"Surely in the Lord I have righteousness and strength.
To Him men shall come,
And all shall be ashamed
Who are incensed against Him."
(Isa 45:23–24)

Faith, a Gift, Ensures the Salvation of All the World

So then, just as salvation is not of ourselves, so also faith, which is part of the salvation process, is not of ourselves. So testifies the Romans Letter. Herein is further hope for all the world—to those distant lands, to those far-off shores, to the islands of the sea (see Ps 65:2, 5, 8). To all the wounded and bereft souls of the earth, to the living and to the dead, to the tyrants and abusers who have yet to be humbled. God is able. "Behold, I am the LORD, the God of all flesh. Is there anything too hard for Me?" (Jer 32:27). Our God who saves is the "God who gives life to the dead and calls into existence the things that do not exist" (Rom 4:17 ESV)—even our faith.

Thus, another shaft of light from the good news pierces our doubt to assure us that God will not fail in fulfilling his irrevocable oath. Just as he took the judgment of all humanity upon himself in his burning, passionate love for the world, just as he justifies all mankind in the righteousness of his Son who sacrificed himself for us, so he also *is able and will* provide humanity with the faith that pushes through the steely mesh of our fears and enters into "the glorious liberty of the children of God" (Rom 8:21).

Faith then, it is clear from the book of Romans, is not a description of the *limits* of salvation (that is, "only to those who have faith"). It is a description of one of the *ingredients* of salvation (that is, "it comes by faith")—what is technically called a *sine qua non* (a "not without which"). Thus, it has within it the element of *inclusiveness*, not exclusiveness, and this is why Paul can say, "We conclude that a man is justified by faith. . . . *Or is He the God of the Jews only?*" (Rom 3:28–29). And, "The faithfulness of Jesus . . . for all who believe. *For there is no distinction among people since all have sinned*" (Rom 3:22–23 ISV). These telling little steps of logic that Paul brings to us make it clear what he's driving at. Faith is not the ingredient that describes the limits of salvation. It is the ingredient that describes the *extensiveness* of salvation. Faith is not the demarcation of the banks where the river ends. It is the description of the river's powerful overflow of the banks that ultimately nurtures the whole land.

And now we must look at something extraordinary by any measure. We have seen that faith is a gift from God. But how does God go about getting mankind's attention enough to confer it?

What circumstances does he skillfully employ to get that faith into the human heart?

Chapter 5

The Witness of Faith (2)//
How God Brings Faith to All Humanity

ONE OF THE WONDERS about God is that he didn't let Adam perish and just start his creation all over again. There are more reasons than humans can fathom why God chose not to take that course of action. Of one, though, we're certain. Adam and his beloved wife lost trust in God, and God was set on restoring their trust in him (Gen 3:21) and in the hearts of all humanity (Isa 45:22).

Letting mankind live, and under the most harrowing circumstances of sin and death, reveals an intriguing aspect of God's plan for mankind. From a human point of view, God's taking a huge gamble. The world's awash with pain and sorrow. The tally of history's colossal feast of suffering and misery is beyond measure. And yet God lets it play out?

An accusing world is likely to interpret this as an expression of God's indifference towards suffering humanity. Anger and dismissive unbelief towards him inevitably pile up throughout the ages as this macabre human performance drags on. But, even without the gospel, this prolongation of mankind's tragedy suggests hope—God has not given up on the human race. And *with* the gospel God has made it clear that he's taken the final judgment of mankind upon himself in Jesus Christ, and faith, therefore, sees his incomprehensible love for human beings and the divine plan for their rescue.

God's ways of doing things never cease to be a scandal to humanity. He doesn't toe the line. His works upset the world's idea of moral order. He doesn't always "save" in the conventional Christian understanding of that word. Far from dispensing with the human race and replacing it with another, and far from protecting his reputation by hushing up the loss and starting over, God moves upon this broken humanity with astonishing mystery *by entangling himself with its sinfulness to create faith in him in the very place where humanity has set up its willful unbelief.* Here again we see the suffering of God displayed as he engages himself with the sin and pain of the world. In the midst of the tortured masses all around him, his own suffering identifies with ours and goes even further, *culminating in the death of his Son for the sins of all mankind.* "In all their afflictions He was afflicted" (Isa 63:9).

From Imprisonment to Mercy

Paul summarizes God's plan to get trust in him back into the hearts of mankind in this remarkable statement:

> For God has consigned all to disobedience, that He may have mercy on all. (Rom 11:32 ESV)

Several other translations read as follows:

> God has *imprisoned* all in disobedience so that He may have mercy on all. (CSB)

> God has *shut up* all in disobedience so that He may show mercy to all. (NASB)

> For God has *locked up* all in the prison of unbelief, that upon all alike He may have mercy. (WEY)

In this brief verse, Paul is describing God's bewildering engagement with the world of sin and death throughout history. There's a plan here. Something is done "so that"—*in order that*—something else may be done. God "imprisons" the whole of humanity in disobedience so that (in order that) he may have mercy on all—*not that a few may be saved and the rest be damned for eternity, but that his mercy may be given to everyone.* An examination of the three principal words in this verse and their relation to one another is needed in order to understand the unorthodoxy of God's plan to restore trust in him through the unlikely means of "imprisonment," "disobedience," and "mercy."

Paul has already made clear what this "imprisonment," this "locking up," this "shutting up," means in earlier parts of his letter. In chapter 5 of his Romans Letter he said that through one man (Adam) "sin entered the world, and death through sin," and that death "reigned" (Rom 5:14), just as "sin reigned" (5:21), over all humankind. As I've pointed out in earlier chapters of this volume, Paul's use of the word "reign" (and "dominion" and being "under" sin) in describing the fallen kingdom of Adam in which all humanity lives is intended to express the prisonlike state human beings fell victim to as a result of Adam's sin (see Rom 5:14). Humanity became trapped in the reign of sin-death.

And Paul's observation that we're imprisoned in *disobedience* is highly significant. At the beginning of the Romans Letter, Paul states that "although [humanity] knew God, they did not glorify Him as God" (Rom 1:21). This is the disobedience of unbelief. Mankind embraced Adam's willful unbelief and became imprisoned in it—*trapped in it*. Here is unbelief so entrenched, so unconscious, in its willfulness that it rapidly became second nature to humankind. And from that willful unbelief flows the corruption of all humanity. But there is something even more astonishing about this.

According to the verse, such a human catastrophe—being locked up, trapped in unbelief—didn't simply happen by way of its own, innate dynamic. "God has locked up all in the prison of unbelief." There's divine purpose here. *Man* chooses unbelief. But *God* chooses to imprison him in it with an aim in mind: *so that he might have*—yes, astonishingly—*mercy on them eventually*. What relationship, then, is there between imprisoning mankind in disobedience and finally being merciful to all?

This idea of being imprisoned and God himself doing the imprisoning takes us back to the beginning of Paul's Romans Letter. Following the disclosure of mankind's universal suppression of God (see Rom 1:18), the letter then describes God's interaction with his fallen creation.

When God "Gives Humans Over," What Is His Intention?

Rather than somehow preventing humans from sinning—putting the brakes on mankind's willful unbelief—he decisively "gave them [all humanity] over"—the wording is repeated three times—to the various forms of idolatry and sins that they had chosen instead of God himself (see Rom 1:24, 26, 28). God doesn't stay humanity's hand. He doesn't attempt to allay

His creatures' plunge into unbelief. He surrenders them to it, handing the world over to these absurd and cruel alternatives of him, *to the things they choose instead of trusting in him* (vv. 24, 26, 28). It is clearly a wrenching divine act of submitting humanity to the consequences of their choice to suppress their trust in him.

It would be a massive theological mistake (though, regrettably, the bird has long since flown) to assume that God is engaged here in providing humanity with a historic "learning moment," as if somehow by God's giving humanity over to its suppression of him he is educating mankind, by its error, to turn and reform itself and follow a different course. That view may be the stuff of Christian humanism, but it's not the gospel.

We have to do a mental U-turn as we come to learn that when God gives humanity over, he doesn't stop with surrendering them to their idols along with the sins that flood the world through them. He also entraps humanity in their idol obsession by use of his law. God actually hands humanity over *to the bondage of his law*. This is a shocking dynamic.

The Romans Letter teaches that far from God's law pulling humanity up short and stemming the tide of sin, *the law creates a profoundly disturbing consciousness of sin that actually causes sin to spread far and wide* (Rom 3:19–20; 7:5, 8, 11, 13). "By the law is the knowledge of *sin*," not righteousness. Confronted by God's law in its conscience (Rom 2:14–15), fallen humanity's relationship to it immediately becomes so dysfunctional that when the human heart attempts to comply with God's law, psychological stress ensues that creates the opposite effect: the *stimulation of passions*. Thus, Paul shockingly speaks of "sinful passions *which were aroused by the law*" (Rom 7:5, 8, 11, 13) and sin, *by the commandment*, producing in him all manner of evil desire (see Rom 7:8).

The gospel in the Romans Letter reveals that the law was never meant to make mankind righteous. The only righteousness that counts—Christ's— is revealed "*apart from the law*" (Rom 3:21). Paul boldly treats the law of God as belonging to the sin kingdom of Adam, even though the law itself is "holy and just and good" (Rom 7:12). In another one of Paul's letters he says, "If righteousness comes through the law then Christ died in vain" (Gal 2:21). And here in his Romans Letter Paul devotes the whole of his seventh chapter explaining that life in the kingdom of grace is, in part, *deliverance* from the law, being *dead* to it. "Therefore . . . you also have become dead to the law. . . . We have been delivered from the law" (Rom 7:4, 6). Dead to the law of God? Delivered from the law that God gave in the first place? Then why did he give it?

When God's law meets the lusts of human idolatry, repressed emotional panic never fails to follow. The cat's thrown among the pigeons. There's a flurry of fur and feathers as our idolatries clash with the spirit of law in our minds. Issues of guilt and "right-doing" and wrongdoing become a preoccupation. We become obsessed by what we fear. And we fear the condemnation of the law in our minds. The irony is that this mental state causes us to be driven to even more law-consciousness with a fixation which we cannot break away from. Paul describes this mental state as "the flesh lust[ing] against the spirit" (Gal 5:17). The book of Genesis describes it as the "enmity" that God puts between the serpent and the woman (Gen 3:15). Psychologists refer to it as cognitive dissonance—that mental crisis in which our values and convictions (cognition) conflict with our behaviors (our lusts and sins), creating an unsettling disharmony in the psyche. The stress of the dissonance leads either to more idolatry to escape the stress, or to the spiritual breaking point: the soul's cry from the darkness of its abyss,

Oh wretched man that I am! (Rom 7:24)

Depart from me, for I am a sinful man, O Lord! (Luke 5:8)

Woe is me, for I am undone! (Isa 6:5)

Thus, mankind is imprisoned in sin by the internal operations of the law within their heart, that law that taunts us in our mind with accusations like, "What's wrong with you?" "You can never do anything right!" "You'll never measure up!" "You're no good!" This is the point at which the mind meets the end of itself and the heart is ready to receive God's gift of faith in his merciful grace in Christ. Handing humanity over to the tyranny of idolatry and law is God's strange act of positioning mankind for the reception of faith—faith in his mercy. "The LORD, the LORD God, merciful and gracious, longsuffering, and abounding in goodness and truth" (Exod 34:6). God "delights in mercy" (Mic 7:18). "He does not retain His anger forever" (Mic 7:18). If he is the author of faith, if he knows how to position mankind to receive it, will he not give what he delights in to *all*?

All the ends of the world
Shall remember and turn to the LORD,
And all the families of the nations
Shall worship before You.
(Ps 22:27)

Throughout the centuries, many theologians and preachers have, with tragic disregard for the overall context and message of the Romans Letter, interpreted God's act of "giving people over" as a pronouncement of damnation, a giving up on sinners—God washing his hands of them and abandoning them to hell. This interpretation is not merely radically different from the one presented in this book. It is, in light of the thematic structure of the Romans Letter, interpretively impossible. It contradicts bold lines of thought, several of which we have already seen Paul has etched into the minds of his readers, thus making the internal message of the Romans Letter quite incoherent. Furthermore, it is entirely contrary to the character of God revealed in the gospel in Romans. And, lastly, its impact is to ride roughshod over the gloriousness of God's irrevocable oath that before him all creatures of humanity will ultimately swear their allegiance, seeing in him only their righteousness and strength.

The gospel message in the Romans Letter clearly shows that when God gives people over, he's not abandoning them to the damnation of hell but setting them, personally and historically, on a *crisis-trajectory*: the unveiling of *his* righteousness in Christ in contrast to their supposed human righteousness (Rom 3:21–22). And that, the letter reveals, leads to justification and life in Christ for all humankind (Rom 5:18). This is the same process that's later described in the verse we're considering: God locking humanity up in willful unbelief—trapping them in it—to lead them ultimately to his mercy toward them (Rom 11:32). The divine trajectory is (a) *giving over*, (b) resulting in ultimate *human loss*, (c) leading to *the revelation of Christ's righteousness*, (d) leading to *justification for all*, (e) leading to *mercy upon all mankind*.

God's goal, then, in giving the world over to the results of their suppression of him is to bring humanity to the stark realization that the world is in *a death-spiral that cannot be halted*. Nor can it be reversed. The salvation God has planned for the human race is not a renovation. It's not an overhaul, a makeover, a cleansing process. It's a death of this natural humanity. The kingdom of Adam will not make it through to eternity. Only a new creation formed in and through the resurrected life of Christ will. "The *whole creation* groans and labors with *birth pangs* together until now" (Rom 8:22). That means the whole creation is in the pains of being reborn. A new creation is envisioned, a new creation not in the sense of a spiritual renewal in individual hearts now (that, of course, is a foretoken of what's to come, a foretaste of it—the firstfruits of the Spirit, Rom 8:23) but a literal re-creation of the whole of humanity where this corruptible must put on incorruption, and this mortal must put on immortality (see 1 Cor 15:51–53). "Behold, I make all things new" (Rev 21:5). Not, "I will make lots of new things and get rid of the rest." No, *all things that now exist*, he will make new. And *all* things will be made new, not just some. And all things will be made *new*, not merely renovated. Jesus' resurrection pronounces the commencement of new life *in him* for the human race. His death pronounces the end of that fallen race in its present condition.

When the grieving heart of God (see Jer 2:5) gives the world over to its idolatrous alternatives to himself, those choices, as they are allowed to follow their inevitable path, gradually bring each soul to the end of its resources, its intended destination: *spiritual emptiness*. We have all known it to some extent: the disappointments of life, the loneliness and depression, tragic circumstances of birth and childhood, the cruel hand of poverty, the loss of a loved one, health crises, or horrendous injustice at the hands of others, or by the abuse of our own selves.

We see the results of humanity's choices throughout history—even beyond the vast political and societal upheavals—in people's endless attempts to satisfy cravings of the heart and mind that have emerged as substitute yearnings for the one, true longing persistently suppressed by unbelief: the precious love and comfort of our eternal Father. Mankind thus enters a fruitless round of spiritual enslavement—fruitless and circular because, by its denial, it misidentifies the problem and throws solutions at it as powerless as snowballs at an oncoming tank. Humanity's *idols* unveil the world's empty heart. God's *law*, by its infliction of guilt and shame, brings it to breaking point. And "a broken and a contrite heart—these, O God, You will not despise" (Ps 51:17).

Thus, God's act of "giving mankind over" is critically necessary in leading humanity *beyond its emptiness to the final goal of his mercy upon every soul*. "For I won't accuse forever, nor will I always be angry; for then the human spirit would grow faint before me—even the souls that I have created" (Isa 57:16 ISV). What catches humanity off balance is God's long-suffering action of involving himself—interjecting himself—into men and women's sinful state of unbelief in such ways as to *hedge up and redirect the results of their folly so that each one may be brought to face the psychic void and feel the tremors beneath them, at which point their hearts are made available to receive the news of mercy from the God they have previously suppressed in their hearts.*

Faith Enters the Soul's Void

It is then, and only then, that God gets faith in him into the hearts of humanity. Faith, therefore, clearly not emerging from some enlightened quality within humanity, comes from above and enters the soul's void where, in its crisis, it has seen the terror of the end of all things.

Hence, since faith is a gift of God and enters our darkness—and all are darkened—then the way is opened for all mankind to receive his merciful gift of faith. And so, it can be truly said, "Where sin abounded, grace abounded *much more*" (Rom 5:20). Is there any place on earth where sin does not abound? Then there is no place on earth where grace does not ultimately abound much more—even to the lowest depths and places of human darkness.

> If I say, "Surely the darkness will overwhelm me, . . ."
> Even the darkness is not dark to You,
> And the night is as bright as the day.
> Darkness and light are alike to You.
> (Ps 139:11–12 NASB)

But why does it have to be this way? Why does God have to take us all the way to our depths before we can know him? The reason is in the nature of sin itself. The sin-kingdom of Adam has created wholesale delusion. Humanity exists in peril of its being, yet is every inch blind to the fact. Only a revelation of that inner peril will open eyes to God's gift of trust in him. Humans are like fish in a fishbowl, trying to comprehend they're wet. We are so immersed in Adam's kingdom of sin and death that we're immune to the stench of its decay. Willful unbelief has wreaked havoc with our minds. It's the *fool* that says in his heart, "There is no God" (Ps 14:1). And the proud show little hesitation in expressing what's on the tip of their tongue: "How does God know? And is there knowledge in the Most High?" (Ps 73:11). The forbidden fruit, pleasant to the eyes, dupes us into thinking it will make us stand out in the crowd (see Gen 3:6; Rom 1:22). Existence in this poisonous state has become so familiar to us that we're mindless of its fatal independence, its mirage of human sovereignty, its tendency to strut around as if we owned the planet—the propensity to live our lives forgetful that the next heartbeat, the next breath, is on loan from God. And all the while, out of God's aching heart come the words, "I myself taught Israel how to walk, leading him along by the hand. But he doesn't know or even care that it was I who took care of him" (Hos 11:3 NLT). It is an independence lethal to the soul, as lethal as odorless gas in a coal mine.

Consequently, faith in God can only make sense to us *in the context of personal and pervasive disorder and loss*. We hear the crack of the branch snapping loose from the tree. The soul is draining dry of self-confidence. Fading in the distance are its claims of spiritual "potential." The heart is exhausted by its endeavors to win life for itself. Spiritual efforts to force an "emptying" of the self, feats of religious austerity, and the vain reach towards transcendence are all shriveling twigs. The soul cannot even contribute to its own emptiness, let alone its fullness. Religion and morality, those sweet angels of darkness, have severed all hope, killing every aspiration to spiritual excellence. Here, in the dead timber of the soul, God plants the life-giving sap of faith.

Since faith is the realization that without God the heart has nowhere else to go but the gutter of despair, and that in Christ alone is the warm, bright hearth of home, God's plan is to let humanity run out the clock of its reputed invincibility until that void, unveiled, stares it in the face. Then emerges poverty of spirit, the advanced stages of soul-starvation. *Here is humanity, positioned for faith, that God might be merciful to all his floundering sheep.*

The Call to Faith Is the Gift of Faith

Then it is that those tender words of Jesus surprise the senses: "Blessed are the poor in spirit. For theirs is the kingdom of heaven" (Matt 5:3). Poverty of spirit, without the gospel, is a psychic terror. But when God's grace reaches into its emptiness, the shivering soul receives its first warm embrace. People whose spiritual strength has been pummeled and sapped by the ravages of their lives and of this world unconsciously long for God's strong, merciful hand to intervene—these are the poor in spirit. Yet, few realize it.

The reality is that *all* are poor in spirit. And therefore, the promise and the assurance are for all. When the full force of being given over to the dismal duo of idolatry and law is realized in the world and in the final judgment, then everyone will become all too aware that they are poor in spirit. Then it is that every knee will bow before his mercy, and every tongue will swear allegiance that in the LORD alone is their source of all goodness and power to live.

So, with this background we can understand Jesus' and his followers' urgent calls to faith more accurately. Verses abound, appearing to suggest that faith comes from humanity's side—that *they* create it.

> The kingdom of God is at hand. Repent and believe in the gospel. (Mark 1:15)

> Your faith has saved you. Go in peace. (Luke 7:50)

> He who has ears to hear, let him hear. (Matt 13:9)

> John . . . baptized . . . saying . . . that they should believe on . . . Christ. (Acts 19:4)

> If you . . . believe . . . you will be saved. (Rom 10:9)

> We implore you, on Christ's behalf, be reconciled to God. (2 Cor 5:20)

> And this is His commandment . . . believe on the name of His Son. (1 John 3:23)

> He who does not believe is condemned . . . because he has not believed. (John 3:18)

> He who comes to God must believe. (Heb 11:6)

> Let us draw near with a true heart in full assurance of faith. (Heb 10:22)

> Beware . . . lest there be in any of you an evil heart of unbelief. (Heb 3:12)

> Whoever desires, let him take the water of life freely. (Rev 22:17)

But in the previous chapter of this volume we saw that a person is described as being justified—declared innocent—by God's grace, justified by Christ's blood, justified by faith. We saw that if it is God who justifies and Christ's sacrificial death that justifies, then for faith to justify as well must mean that it, too, comes from God just as God's grace and Christ's sacrifice do. We saw that the "righteousness of faith" is a phrase that indicates that faith is from God because, in the first place, it is a righteousness—a quality which human beings do not innately possess—and, in the second place, it is imputed—charged to a person's account by God, and therefore it is not coming from the human side.

So how can the verses above, and many others like them, be understood as faith coming from God's side when they appeal to humans to believe as if faith were to come from their side?

Reality is redefined in the presence of Jesus. When Jesus enters the world and declares the kingdom of grace to mankind, there, in that moment, is *the creative act and a world of grace operating over and above—and into—this world*. God, in the presence of Jesus, is in the process of bringing faith to life in the hearts of human beings. The appeals from Jesus and his representatives—"Repent and believe," "Your faith has healed you," "Be reconciled to God," "Hear if you have ears," "Believe in the Lord Jesus Christ," "If you believe you will be saved," "God's commandment is that you believe," "You must believe that God is a Rewarder," "Draw near to him with a true heart," "Beware of an evil heart of unbelief," "Take the water of life"—all these are God's moments of his kingdom breaking into our human kingdoms, of God implementing his work of faith in human beings who have been positioned by instilling in them the desire and the capacity to trust in him. *In the grace-command is the faith-enablement. In the appeal is the creative moment.*

When Jesus calls for faith, he is the Creator-Redeemer engaged in summoning that faith, a faith that brings life into the nothingness of sin and death. That's why Paul, in his chapter on Abraham, equates the birth of faith in Christ with God's power to raise the dead: "It shall be imputed to us who believe in Him who raised up Jesus our Lord from the dead" (Rom 4:24).

Yes, Paul isn't done with the life of Abraham yet. The most convincing argument for faith coming from God and being seeded in a human by God himself when a person reaches his nothingness is made plain in the life of this extraordinary human being.

Abraham's Encounter: Proof That Faith Is a Gift from God

Isolated from the crowd by enormous wealth and power, Abraham might have given off an air of idiosyncrasy, as the "great" of this world often do. He'd believed for years that he'd be the father of nations (Gen 12:2–3). He'd even changed his name at the age of ninety-nine from Abram (meaning "lord") to Abraham (meaning "father of a multitude"; Gen 17:5).

It's not hard to imagine the day he asked his household and neighbors to call him Abraham from then on, many of them looking on, cloaking a wry smile, assuming that he meant well, and putting it all down to his aging mind. And without doubt the news would have gotten to the local inn that he had cut off the foreskin of his penis and ordered all male members of his hundreds-strong household to do the same as a sign of faith in God's covenant, a sign possibly meant to convey that when it comes to God's promise, male potency won't do the trick.

It was about a child, you see. He and his wife, Sarah, had no child together, and yet he had this belief that he'd be the father of all families of the earth. Sarah was barren. They'd tried for years with no success. The humiliation must have weighed heavily on Abraham in that patriarchal age. He had everything this world could offer *except the one thing that counted*, the one thing he was powerless to produce. In a few vivid verses Paul catches the painful beauty of Abraham's life of faith. He "considered his own body, which was as good as dead (since he was about a hundred years old)" (Rom 4:19 ESV). Yet, "contrary to hope, in hope [he] believed" (Rom 4:18).

Because God had appeared to Abram twenty-five years earlier and stirred up the empty nest by some startlingly good news. God had given him a promise when he was seventy-five, telling him he'd become a great nation, that through his offspring all families of the earth would be blessed, and God would give his descendants the land of Canaan (see Gen 12:2–3, 7). At seventy-five? And married to a sixty-five-year-old wife who was barren?

At this point we run the risk of reading the account of Abraham's life through the sieve of our modern, secular Christian thought, with its tendency to think of faith as an act initiated by the human will. But the writer of his history makes no attempt to portray Abraham as some superhero of faith sallying forth to conquer the world. In fact, the principal character in this drama is not Abraham. It's God.

Abraham's brave act of responding to God's command to leave his home for another land was undoubtedly faith in its fledgling state, vulnerable to the predators of self-doubt, for the account shows him making one blunder after another in his attempts to keep himself alive, as if God needed his help to fulfill his promise. And the writer of Genesis makes no bones about recording the blunders. To the contrary, he goes out of his way to show how every fiber of Abraham's being revolts against faith as if it were (as it is!) a foreign body he's instinctively trying to reject.

The Witness of Faith (2)

He flees from Canaan—the very land God called him to settle in—to seek refuge in Egypt, away from the warlike tribes and famine in Canaan (Gen 12:6, 10). He embarrasses himself and his vast company by lying to Pharaoh about his wife in order to save his own skin, only to be expelled from the land under armed guard (Gen 12:11-20). The humiliation compels him to go back to the place where God first appeared to him to remind himself of God's promise (Gen 13:1-4).

And while all this is going on, Abraham and Sarah in their intimate moments are trying to make a child together. The efforts over a decade are so exasperating that Abraham whines to God, "Look, You have given me no offspring" and suggests that Eleazar should be his heir (Gen 15:2-3). Not much later, exasperation swells to desperation, and Abraham and his wife agree that he should try for a child through Sarah's handmaid, Hagar (Gen 16:1-4). Hence the skirting of the promise and the birth of Ishmael. And even when Abraham reaches ninety-nine and God assures him of a son through Sarah, Abraham pleads, "Oh that Ishmael might live before You!" (Gen 17:18).

Yet through all these faith-gaffes God is gentle with Abraham and keeps repeating his promise to him, thereby instilling faith in him in the very midst of his doubts. "Lift up your eyes... northward, southward, eastward, and westward, for all the land which you see I will give you" (Gen 13:14-15). "I will make your descendants as the dust of the earth" (Gen 13:16). "Do not be afraid, Abram. I am your shield, your exceedingly great reward" (Gen 15:1). "Look toward heaven and count the stars if you are able.... So shall your descendants be" (Gen 15:5). For a moment, Abram believes again after another bout of doubt, and the LORD "accounted it to him for righteousness" (Gen 15:6). But not long after, he seems overwhelmed once more and cries out before him, "Lord GOD, how shall I know that I will inherit it?" (Gen 15:8).

Faith from above weighs heavy on the shoulders of this aging man. But the LORD, having gotten Abram where he wants him, now provides him with more specifics. *Enact a covenant. Sarah, your wife, will bear you a son this time next year. Circumcise yourself. Call his name Isaac* (see Gen 17). The fullness of faith now floats lightly down upon Abram like a feather. The light dawns. He sees now what it all means: it's *God's* work (the covenant!). "This child won't come from my potency!" After all, then, the sense of faith's *heaviness* had come from Abraham's resistance to it.

Faith itself is no burden when the soul is ready for it. It is the gentle wind of God's breath. And now Abraham was ready to breathe it in! He had come to the end of himself. He faced the fact that his body was as good as dead. In the light of God's new specifics, he was open to receiving God's initiative. He clung to a hope beyond all hope. He believed now in the God "who calls those things which do not exist as though they did" (Rom 4:17). It's as if he might have said, "If this is going to happen, it'll have to be a miracle!" And perhaps God had been waiting in the wings for twenty-four years, gradually bringing him to realize that. Abraham, a little giddy at the realization, laughed at the irony of it all (Gen 17:17). Moments later, God, not to let the humor go to waste, gently prods him by telling him to name the child Isaac.

"Isaac" means "laughter."

Here is God at his best. Planning joy out of sorrow, vigor out of weariness, hope out of despair, faith out of doubt, life out of death, abundance out of want—and happy trouble out of deathly tedium. Can anyone doubt that this is the story of the Creator-Redeemer bringing the life of faith into dead things?

Abraham and Sarah's chuckles rippled on through the following year, and all her friends shared in the laughter at the idea of Sarah, furrowed as an old prune at ninety, having a baby, and her hundred-year-old husband, wizened as a walnut, looking on with jovial pride (see Gen 21:5–6).

Strange indeed, then, that Paul should say Abraham "did not waver at the promise of God through unbelief" (Rom 4:20). Paul, please! He wavered at almost every turn in the story! What are you talking about?! But Paul was looking from the top down—from God's actions—not from the bottom up—not from Abraham's actions. God was the hero here. It was *God's gift of faith* that was not wavering, no matter how many doubts Abraham struggled with. It was God who *imputed* faith to Abraham—treated it as though it came from Abraham. It was God who acted as if (imputed) it was a righteousness coming from Abraham, when in fact it was God treating him so. This is the faith that doesn't waver because God does not fail in giving it and shoring it up through all the ups and downs of life. Abraham was buckling under it, but when, through the years, he was finally brought to the end of hope, the hope that faith brought made him laugh. "Abraham believed God, and it was accounted to him for righteousness" (Rom 4:3).

The Witness of Faith (2)

Faith: The Gift of Life in Our Spiritual Death

So just as God instilled faith in Abraham, so also when Jesus declares, "Your faith has saved you," and "Your faith has healed you," these are not mere words. "The words that I speak to you . . . *are life*" (John 6:63). They are words breathing life into spiritual deadness, into souls that have been burned out on idolatrous despair, made more formidable by obsession with law, so that when his words are heard the soul's brokenness is already sufficiently shattered as to end its resistance; and there is a rattling, and dead bones come together, bone upon bone, and breath comes back into the soul (see Ezek 37:7–14). And when that happens, even though the faith in the soul is created by the breath of Jesus' Spirit, it is created in *humans*, and therefore Jesus has the graciousness to speak of that faith as if it originated in humanity.

It is Jesus' aim to let people know that *they* are the ones believing because the faith that he gives doesn't make a detour around the mind. Instead, it activates it in view if its existential collapse. Rather than bypassing a person's mental faculties and creating something that is not the self, Jesus makes humans know their humanity *by the revelation of who they are in him* so that even though still in a fallen, imperfect state, people find their personalities revitalized by trusting in Almighty God in Christ, and thus they act with a new freedom as individuals before God, accounted in Christ's image.

How, for example, shall we understand the raising of Lazarus? When Jesus called out, "Lazarus come forth!" (John 11:43), was he speaking into some living part of Lazarus that could hear the command? No, dead Lazarus was *lifeless*. Jesus' command didn't need a vestige of Lazarus to continue its existence in order to hear what Jesus was calling him to do. That, possibly, was one of the reasons why Jesus held back until Lazarus had been dead four days. Lazarus had to be seen as not simply dead but *rotting* (John 11:39) so that the bystanders could know that Jesus' call to *life* was a creation-from-nothing, activated by his command, just as God had created life in Sarah's barren body two millennia before—just as God "calls those things which do not exist *as though they did*" (Rom 4:17).

This is how it is with faith. When Jesus calls us to believe the gospel, he is not calling to some spiritual scrap in us that's gasping for breath and therefore still capable of sucking in the wind of his Spirit. He is creating in a person the power to breathe in faith in the instant of his command to believe.

There is a mysterious union between Jesus and those who have faith in him. "Abide in Me, and I in you . . . for without Me you can do nothing" (John 15:4–5). But how can people, who can't do anything without Christ in the first place, initiate abiding in him? To abide is an act of faith. Since without him we're powerless to do anything, then that faith—which is an abiding—must be initiated by Jesus *so that Christ is initiating the abiding in the act of commanding it from us through the faith he gives*. We then continue abiding by his constantly renewing Spirit who regularly "restores [our] soul" (Ps 23:3). Once again, we see here that faith is not a choice of the will emanating from some life within our soul. Rather, faith given by God *awakens* the soul from death (see Eph 2:1, 5) and enables it to *will* again and to activate the person, though a broken person, in this world.

Similarly when Paul says, "Work out your own salvation . . . for it is God who works in you, both to will and to do for His good pleasure" (Phil 2:12–13), what is the mystery taking place here but that when God works in us, it's a work so respecting and reenergizing the personhood of each individual—not bypassing his identity but establishing it—that *God's* working in us is at the same time *our* working things out. There is an interconnectedness between the Holy Spirit and believers so close that it is hard to define its boundaries. Thus, Jesus tells a believer not to worry about what they should say before the city magistrates because the Holy Spirit "will teach you in that very hour what you ought to say" (Luke 12:12). So, who's doing what here? Is it the Holy Spirit speaking or the believer?

And isn't it common knowledge among Christians that when a believer accomplishes something wonderful, they often feel compelled to say, "I couldn't have done it without God"? In their simplicity, never a truer theological word was spoken. Our gracious God, not short-circuiting the personality and will of a human being but bringing it to life by the gift of faith when it's at its wit's end, establishes us as creations in his image, even though still flawed and sinful.

This, then, is the state of mind and the condition of the world in which faith is created. Not an enlightened society giving birth to faith, not a soul that has had a eureka moment, but one facing the depths of its suffering and loss and spiritual impotence. All other "faith" is a whistling in the dark. It is the faith that *God* gives—*for the LORD alone will be exalted in that day* (Isa 2:11)—that leads to the salvation of all mankind. If it were left to humans to come up with it, they would be running after the wind (see Eccl 5:16 CEV). But with God, it is another matter. "I am like a tree that is always green," he says, "*all* your fruit comes from *Me*" (Hos 14:8 NLT).

The Witness of Faith (2)

Our Ever-Present, Absent God

A strange thing we see, then. The absence of God in humanity is the very evidence of his presence, for that absence is God preparing the soul for his presence. His seeming abandonment is his involvement. The world's *no* to God is God's determined *yes through its no*. While he is gifting faith in some whom he has prepared, he's positioning the rest for faith by preparation. The reception of faith starts with a negative. The *yes* of faith forces its way through the *no* of all our pains. The accumulation of sorrow and loss each person endures in a lifetime, long or short, the grief, loneliness, broken family life, addictions, mental torments, the futility of the daily round, the collapse of life's dreams, the tragedy, the abuse, the searing poverty, the rape of human trafficking, the teeming masses of parentless children, the ravages of war, the stress of safeguarding wealth, the increasing meaninglessness of secular culture, the tyrannies of despotic governments, all are fodder for the blooming of faith—faith that God through Jesus comes close to us all in the voiding pain. And there is plenty of it to go around.

Through his Spirit, God works in every human soul by his intimate interaction with the sin, sorrow, and loss that is choking his creation by its suppression of him. "The LORD looks from heaven; He sees all the sons of men. From the place of His dwelling He looks on all the inhabitants of the earth; He fashions their hearts individually" (Ps 33:13–15). When the world can no longer stand it, when we are desperate to come up for air, when, in the end, every soul finds itself in possession of an indescribable longing for home, Mercy, seeing us from a great way off, runs to meet us. And the soul hardly gets a chance to express its unworthiness before the Father throws his robe of love around it (see Luke 15:21–22).

Such an understanding of the far-reaching nature of grace can be grasped as we believe that God, having taken the final judgment of mankind upon himself, intends to be faithful to his unbreakable oath and save all, as every person, having come to an end of their human resources, bows before him and every tongue swears that in Christ alone is their righteousness and strength.

Faith from Humanity's Side: The Crippling of the Gospel

If, on the other hand, we hold out against that promise and cling to the view that some, by virtue of a supposed blissful independence, initiate salvation by making a *choice* of faith, while the rest *choose not* to initiate faith—and, therefore, some will be saved by stint of an innate quality or willpower-faith while most will be lost by a qualitative deficiency or flaw in that will to have faith—then it's impossible to see how the scriptural teaching of faith links with the equally biblical proclamation of God's salvation of all. Things don't make sense. Truth is strewn all over the floor in bits, and we've no idea where to start picking up the pieces and putting them back together again.

For to believe that some, *of their own initiative*, will believe and others won't, can lead only to one of two ultimate and erroneous conclusions: either there is an ingredient in certain people that makes them capable of overcoming their willful unbelief so that a quality few will be saved (and that makes God's plan of *imprisoning all in disobedience in order to have mercy on all* meaningless); or, God arbitrarily chooses to give faith to some while choosing to discard the rest (and that makes God's act of *taking the final judgment of the world upon himself* invalid, and the love of God, a confusion). A limited salvation, therefore, presupposes a cause either in a hidden human condition that prevents most from believing, or a hidden divine purpose that doesn't allow most to believe.

But we have seen in the chapters of this book so far that this kind of thinking is incompatible with the love and plan of God. It is unbiblical, rationally incoherent, and morally flawed. It is, in fact, wicked. That faith comes from God, and that he alone plants it in the human heart when the heart comes to the end of its resources, is one of the fundamental building blocks of the truth that God's triumphant love through Christ will rescue all his precious creation.

And should we be in any doubt that God brings people to an end of themselves in order to gift them with faith, we need to take another look at Israel.

Chapter 6

The Witness of Ezekiel (1)
Israel's *Unfaithfulness* Testifies
to the Salvation of All

ONE BRIEF, BROAD SWEEP and the curtain has been pulled back to reveal God's intriguing involvement in the history of his creation: "God has *consigned* all to *disobedience*, that he may have *mercy on all*" (Rom 11:32 ESV). So, then, we ought to be able to see Old Testament prophets and events confirming Paul's words.

As the Romans Letter sheds light on Old Testament history, it shouldn't surprise us—though it will—to see that history illuminated with the hope of judgments leading to ultimate life, not permanent doom. Countless Christians have been left confused by the judgments of the Old Testament. They wonder how they square with the gospel. Presumably, the issue is resolved for many by ignoring it. But ignorance is bliss only as long as it's total. And we have just enough peripheral knowledge of the Old Testament to be disturbed by it. *So, in this chapter we'll see how Old Testament judgments are part of the gospel declaration of God's salvation of all humanity.* First, though, a review, to remind ourselves how far-reaching is that short one-liner by Paul: "God has consigned all to disobedience, that he may have mercy on all."

1. We've seen that God promises by an unbreakable oath that before him every knee shall bow and every tongue shall swear that in him alone is their righteousness and strength (Isa 45:23–24). We have seen that this oath is a description of God's redemptive plan because when everyone

bows they will swear that Christ is their righteousness and strength (Rom 14:10–11; Phil 2:9–11). *See the introduction and chapter 1.*

2. We've seen that the gospel proclaims God's passionate love for humanity by his appeasement of his own pained and wrathful judgment against sin and evil, taking it upon himself in the person of his Son (Rom 3:25) and on behalf of all mankind. He therefore pronounces all men and women freed from eternal judgment and reconciled in Christ, even while they are still ungodly and enemies (2 Cor 5:19; Rom 4:5; 5:10). *See chapter 3.*

3. We've seen that the extent of the collapse of Adam's kingdom, which brought condemnation and death to all mankind, is countered by the equal extent of Christ's victorious kingdom, which brought justification—the pronouncement of innocence and life—to all mankind (Rom 5:18). *See chapter 4.*

4. And we've seen that the gospel message is that it is necessary for God to show how humanity's departure from him imprisons them, and thus, to hand over humanity to that imprisonment of willful unbelief in order to position them to embrace his abundant *mercy* (Rom 11:32). *See chapter 2.*

5. Furthermore, we've seen that faith in Christ is *a gift from God*, and doesn't come from the human mind, and that God is able to—and will—position all people to receive it and thereby reconcile all humanity through faith in him through his Son (John 12:32). *See chapters 4 and 5.*

6. So then, it is evident that at long last *every creature in heaven and on the earth and under the earth and such as are in the sea, and all that are in them* (Rev 5:13) will, at the climax of all things, express total confidence in God's sacrificial atonement for them—depicted by the slain Lamb on the throne (Rev 5:6, 13)—and be filled with praise to God the Father and his Son, and, consequently, all human history will be consummated in Christ so that everything in heaven and earth will find its perfection in him (Eph 1:9–10; Col 1:20). *See chapters 2 and 3.*

The Reason Why Judgments Must Lead to Redemption

Since these realities are so clearly stated in the gospel, it is beyond dispute that God's judgments in the Bible, particularly the judgments of the Old Testament, both those prophesied and those meted out, are judgments that, no matter how drastic, will lead to God's far-reaching mercy towards humanity and their eternal life.

In light of the fact that the judgment God took upon himself in Christ for the world's evil is eternal and universal—"*This Man* [Jesus] . . . offered *one sacrifice* for sins forever" (Heb 10:12) which is "an *eternal* redemption" (Heb 9:12) and an "*everlasting* covenant" (Heb 13:20), which he "gave" "for the *world*" (John 3:16)—then, *ipso facto*, the judgments of the Old Testament must have a different purpose—*that of moving sinners in the direction of eternal life*—and cannot mean the ultimate death (by either hell or extinction) since that judgment is taken by God himself in Jesus Christ, his Son (Rom 3:25). Anything short of this strips the glory off that declaration, "Behold the Lamb of God that takes away the sin of the world!" (John 1:29) and leaves it dangling as a mere potential.

To our already preconditioned minds a conclusion like this appears preposterous. Yet it follows from the logic of faith, based, as we have seen, upon the *divinely revealed premises of God's atoning work in Christ*. It is the necessary—indeed compelling—conclusion, given the gospel data that God's word provides. (1) The irrevocable oath, (2) the total countermanding of Adam's kingdom by the kingdom of Christ, and (3) the universal outcome of entrapment in sin resulting in mercy for all—these facts *demand* this boldness of faith in God. Otherwise, things as they stand in our Christian faith come dangerously close to being bogus. The shock we experience faced with this logic, far from arising from faulty premises, stems from the clash of our crimped Christian credos with the faith-logic of Christ's sacrifice for the world. And thus, *mercy* after judgment sounds like a flight into featherbrained cockamamie. But what appears to be the foolishness of God is wiser—and wider—than all the wisdom of men (see 1 Cor 1:25).

So, then, we take the good news of God's plan for us in Christ and let it shine on the meaning of Old Testament judgments. As we do, we discover there's no need to twist verses to fit the New Testament paradigm. God's intention to save all humanity is already there in its infancy (sometimes, fully grown up!) couched in fledgling texts (sometimes, mature verses!) that hint (sometimes they're downright bold) at something more glorious than anything so far conceived but now realized when the magnificence of Christ's sacrifice shines on them. At times light blazes through on its own, as we've seen with God's irrevocable oath, like a luminous flash from deep space, but as it had seemed an anomaly in our limited mental universe, we'd moved on. Now, though, we're ready to let the gospel's radiance highlight the pages of the prophets, sharpening texts that had previously appeared fuzzy. Then God's plan for the salvation of the whole human family is confirmed in the ancient script, brought to full significance through the compassionate death and resurrection of Jesus for every man and woman, every boy and girl.

There are five things we need to take note of as we launch into this Old Testament data.

The Significance of Israel for the World's Salvation

First, it's all about Israel. When we explore Old Testament history involving God's judgments, we soon become aware that Israel is at the center of it all. Her destiny is always in the minds of the prophets. This, of course, isn't surprising to those familiar with the Bible. The book, after all, is a history of the Jews. But from another point of view, it gives us something of a jolt when Jesus, who assures us that "God so loved the *world*" (John 3:16), throws a curve ball with the words "salvation is of the *Jews*" (John 4:22). It cannot be denied, therefore, that God's love for the world is communicated, by words and deeds and finally by *the* Word, Jesus Christ himself, through the Jewish people.

Second, God's judgments on Israel are a window on his judgments on the world. In the light of the gospel, it becomes clear that God's redemptive judgments on Israel reveal what the outcome of similar judgments will be for all humanity. The uniqueness of Israel's call and mission is not that they were chosen from an otherwise rejected humanity, but rather that they were chosen *for the sake of and on behalf of* that humanity. Consider this: What revelation of God's redemptive acts in human history, besides his Son, has he given us other than his dealings with Israel? Where else can we go outside Israel's history that doesn't land us in some other nation's pagan backyard? Israel testifies to the one, true, Almighty God and Redeemer (Isa 43:10–13)—a witness to what the Redeemer does, not only for Israel but, as the Romans Letter puts it, for *the whole creation* which is groaning in anticipation of new birth, waiting to be delivered (see Rom 8:20-22).

That Israel is a representation—a model, a prototype, *the essence*—of how God relates to the rest of humankind is witnessed to everywhere by Christians who read their Bibles and take inspiration and instruction from Israel's history *as if that history were their own* (see 2 Tim 3:16). When we lay our head on our pillow and close our eyes at night and comfort ourselves with the words of a psalm like, "He who keeps you will not slumber; behold, He who keeps Israel shall neither slumber nor sleep" (Ps 121:3-4), we non-Jewish people seem not to give a thought to the fact that the psalm says it's the God of *Israel* who keeps us. Israel, in its brokenness, is a prototype of all humanity living out its brokenness before God. *God, in his mercy, foreshadows his redemption of all humanity through his prototype, Israel.* All the families of the earth are to be blessed through Israel (see Gen 12:3). Thus, as goes Israel, so goes the world.

Third, the forgiveness God provides for Israel is the forgiveness he provides for the world. The atonement is the ultimate and indisputable evidence that as goes Israel, so goes the world. When God declares that he will "remove the iniquity of that land [of Israel] in one day" (Zech 3:9), the gospel makes clear "that land" reaches, in fact, to the ends of the earth. Thus, Zechariah's declaration becomes in the mouth of John the Baptist, "Behold the Lamb of God who takes away the sin of *the world!*" (John 1:29). Isaiah saw the link between Israel and the world clearly. God tells Isaiah to proclaim this about the Messiah: "It is too small a thing that You should be My Servant to raise up the tribes of Jacob and to restore the protected ones of Israel; *I will also make You a light of the nations so that My salvation may reach to the end of the earth*" (Isa 49:6 NASB). Similarly, the Romans Letter declares that "the mystery" of Jesus Christ (the *Jewish* Messiah!) is to be "made known to all nations" (Rom 16:26). God's salvation, therefore, even though it was to become a glorious thing for his people Israel, is to be a light of revelation to all the world also (see Luke 2:32). Says God, of Israel, "Nations shall come to your light, and kings to the brightness of your rising" (Isa 60:3 ESV). And through the prophet Jeremiah, God promises, "At that time Jerusalem shall be called The Throne of the LORD, and all the nations shall be gathered to it, to the name of the LORD, to Jerusalem. No more shall they follow the dictates of their evil hearts" (Jer 3:17).

Fourth, as *all* Israel is saved by the atonement God provides, so is *all* the world by that same atonement. It's not until we realize the thoroughness of God's atonement for Israel—its *absolute effectiveness*; the power of God through the sacrifice of his Son to restore *the whole house of* Israel—that the full significance of this for all humanity dawns on us. The atonement God made for Israel by the suffering Messiah was total—no one is left out, none of the sinners, none of those who had done abominations. God intends to have mercy not merely on a remnant. The "whole house of Israel" is to receive mercy (Ezek 39:25). The whole house of Israel is to receive resurrection (Ezek 37:11–14). The whole house is to be restored (Ezek 36:22–38). Therefore, it is the whole house of Israel that is forgiven for all that they have done (Ezek 16:63). So, since Israel's witness of God's merciful judgments (to them all) is *to* the world and *for* the world, it is the whole world, not just a part of it, that will be forgiven, resurrected, and restored. The parallel before us, as we shall see, is not God's mercy on a remnant of Israel and therefore God's mercy upon a remnant of the world, but rather, God's mercy on the whole house of Israel and therefore God's mercy upon all the world (Rom 11:32). As John so forcefully put it, "We have an advocate with the Father, Jesus Christ the righteous. And He Himself is the propitiation for our sins, *and not for ours only but also for the whole world*" (1 John 2:1–2).

And fifth, God's atoning sacrifice is provided amid humanity's barbarism, as is evidenced by his atonement of Israel (Ezek 16:60–63) amid *their* barbarism—namely, the abominable paganism of human sacrifices to supposedly appease God. This is surely why Paul can say that while we were *without strength, ungodly, sinners,* and *enemies* of God, Christ died for us and reconciled us (see Rom 5:6, 8, 10). Paul didn't come up with this brazen idea out of his own head. He saw it boldly etched in the Old Testament. In the prophets we face the alarming harshness of life. Confronting the brutality in those times (but are those times really much different from our own?) and the judgments that follow, without falling trap to whitewashing the whole scenario, is no easy matter. Even as devoted Christians, the inclination to paper over the cracks presses in. But if the gospel proclamation of God's plan to save all humanity through his Son doesn't embrace an admission of the *barbarism of mankind* and God's harsh judgments against it, and how human cruelty is played out in view of the atoning work of Christ, *then no one will take seriously our claim that God is intent on rescuing all his creation* (Rom 8:21–22). It's not going to look good if others perceive we've slid into summer lullabies about God's salvation of all by pie-in-the-sky theology that neatly ignores the conundrum of what God does with human evil. In that case this book would be written off as a pipe dream.

That God will have mercy on all must be allowed its full shock value as it is viewed before the backdrop of the unspeakable callousness humanity is capable of. Faith in God—*our bewildering God!*—is a brave thing. It has the courage to believe that it's precisely because of the meekness and lowliness of God Most High that he brings judgments upon the cruel pride of a human race that inflicts harm on its own kind (see Isa 57:15). No theology of the salvation of all mankind can pass muster, and certainly not grip the minds of serious Christians, if it doesn't face up to God's *interaction* with humankind's darkest horrors in his determination to bring about its rescue.

Israel's Abandonment of God

And so, as we turn the pages of Israel's ancient history, we see that God set her "in the midst of the nations and the countries all around her" (Ezek 5:5). She was called to "blossom and bud, and fill the face of the world with fruit" (Isa 27:6). He rescued her from bondage and enemies *"that all the kingdoms of the earth may know that You are the LORD, You alone"* (Isa 37:20). But, tragically, Israel's fruit soured, and she turned out to do "wickedness more than the nations" (Ezek 5:6).

The catalogue of ancient Israel's corruption beggars belief. Israel "set their abominations in the house which is called by My name" (Jer 7:30). There, in the temple, graffiti of god-animals and crawling things, most likely related to Egyptian pagan worship, was scrawled all around on the walls (Ezek 8:10). Seventy of the elders of the country were standing in front of the wall art, each with a censer in his hand, thick clouds of incense going up to these idols (Ezek 8:11–12). And in their harebrained thoughts they said to themselves, "The LORD doesn't see. He's forsaken the land" (see v. 12).

As if that weren't enough, twenty-five other men in the inner court of God's house had their backs to the temple, facing east, bowing down worshiping the sun (Ezek 8:16). At the north gate of the temple, women sat weeping for Tammuz (Ezek 8:14), presumably the Greek god Adonis, beloved husband of Venus, whose death women grieved over annually, followed by celebrations over his supposed resurrection. Pagan shrines stood at the head of every road. "High places" decked out in colorful cloths were built on every street (Ezek 16:16, 31; Jer 11:13). They made for themselves male idols so that Israel could "play the harlot on them" (Ezek 16:17). Utterly unhinged prophets abounded—magicians, more like, for "the prophet is a fool" (Hos 9:7)—wearing charms, covered in veils, hunting souls like birds, pronouncing empty visions, spouting delusional oracles that made good people sad and bad people happy (Ezek 13:20–23). Israel was overwhelmed by the temptation to fit in with surrounding cultures in a frantic reach for help to resist invaders wherever they could get it. "We want to be like the nations, like the peoples of the world, who serve wood and stone" (Ezek 20:32 NIV). So went the thoughts of their mind. The Babylonians, who "gather captives like sand" (Hab 1:9), were at the gates. Israel made an alliance with Egypt. Taking on her gods may have been part of the bargain. So desperate had the nation become that she offered herself for spiritual harlotry to anyone who would accept—the Egyptians, the Assyrians, the Chaldeans. The scandal made even the Philistines ashamed of the goings on they heard about in Israel. "How degenerate is your heart," the LORD said (Ezek 16:26–30).

We're reading here in Ezekiel of the collapse of a civilization. Social order was in free fall. The people had lost their center in God and hence the center of their society and their reason for being. Idol worship of all varieties gradually introduced a state of dehumanization. The insight of an earlier generation expressed it precisely: "Their idols are silver and gold, the work of men's hands, they have mouths, but do not speak; eyes they have, but they do not see. . . . *Those who make them are like them*" (Ps 115:4–5, 8). Israel's images were nothing more than a projection of a soulless, cruel self. Her idolatry went hand in hand with shedding blood (Ezek 33:25). She filled the place with the blood of the innocents (Ezek 33:25; Jer 19:4). Instead of relying on her Redeemer she relied on the sword (Ezek 33:26), and thus violence filled the land (Ezek 8:17). The princes of Israel had become like wolves tearing the prey, an ancient mafia destroying people for the sake of money (Ezek 22:27), using their power to kill (Ezek 22:6). People of the land followed suit, oppressing each other, committing robbery, mistreating the poor and needy, grinding down the stranger (Ezek 22:29). They made light of their fathers and mothers and mistreated the fatherless and widows (Ezek 22:7). Men slandered and bribed as a ploy to commit murder (Ezek 22:9, 12). They made profit from their neighbors by extortion (Ezek 22:11–12), and of course, sex was never absent from the mix—with a neighbor, with a daughter-in-law, with a sister (Ezek 22:11), debasing one another's wives (Ezek 33:26). They "have forgotten Me," said the LORD God (Ezek 22:12).

Desperate to get some answers from their alternative not-gods, they descended into their own self-created hell. In the valley of Tophet (Jer

7:31), just over the walls of Jerusalem's western and southern limits, their demented minds led them to crazed attempts to appease their not-gods by sacrificing their little children in the fire in distraught pleas for help against their enemies (Ezek 16:20–21, 36; 20:26, 31; 23:37, 39). Some scholars believe that the word *tophet* comes from a word meaning "drum." Supposedly the priests banged drums so that the screams of the little ones would not be heard as they were cast into the fiery mouths of the pagan not-gods, Moloch and Baal. But there are other possibilities for the origin of this word, so its meaning is uncertain. What is not uncertain is that leaders of the nation officiated in what came to be known as this Valley of Slaughter (Jer 7:32).

Divine Direction Behind Disaster

Here, though, we must come to an abrupt halt. Almost certainly, as we read the paragraphs above, our thinking process slipped into its default mode: "Ah, God had a good plan originally. But Israel blew it. What a disaster." I remember thinking this myself when I read the Bible for the first time as a boy of fifteen. In fact, the words I wrote six paragraphs ago, that God set Israel in the midst of the nations to bud and blossom and fill the earth with fruit, but tragically Israel's fruit soured and she did worse than all the other nations, those words I penned may have been the very moment our default mode of thinking kicked in. That word "tragically" might suggest something unforeseen happened—as if God's plan hit an unexpected roadblock.

But this understanding of Old Testament history is as different from the gospel as chalk and cheese. The lumps look alike. But it takes only a bit of poking to clue us in to the fact that we're on to the wrong thing. Israel's ancient corruption was no accident, no unanticipated spoke in the wheel. The gospel overview of Israel's history is clear: *God, in an Almighty act of his sovereignty, gave Israel and the nations up to their idols* (see Rom 1:24, 26, 28). It's here that the tragedy lies. If our Almighty God and Father is to save his creation from itself, he must, in deep turmoil of heart, show humanity the dreadful effects of deserting him, followed by his incredible grace of rescuing them. The primary mover, therefore, in Israel's idolatry is God, not humanity. Yet, there is no fatalism here.

Humankind chose their lifeless idols because they *un*-chose their eternal Creator and life-giver (see Ps 36:9). And the point is, God chose not to stop them but to hedge in their recklessness so that it would fall out only in God-ordained directions. The urge to worship God has an internal pull so strong that when it is repressed the drive to worship alternatives becomes inversely irrepressible. Jeremiah described it to a tee: "My people have committed two evils: they have forsaken Me, the fountain of living waters, and [consequently?] hewn themselves cisterns—broken cisterns that can hold no water" (Jer 2:13). "Think it over and see how evil and bitter it is for you to abandon the LORD your God and to have no fear of Me" (Jer 2:19 CSB). God is not one option among many. He is the very fountain of life (see Ps 36). There is no God besides him (see Isa 44:8). And the presence of universal idolatry in ancient Israel only goes to show that humanity's drive to worship Almighty God is so innate and irresistible that when it is blocked it *must* resurface, but it does so in grotesque deformities that make a mockery of all that is truly human—and divine. All those who hate him, inadvertently, therefore "love death" (Prov 8:36).

Hence the dreadful onslaught.

God Moves upon Israel

Ezekiel, a young married priest, had been part of a mass deportation when Babylon, "more fierce than evening wolves" (Hab 1:8), made its first of three assaults on Jerusalem, in 589 BC. A decade later the LORD told Ezekiel that the "desire of [his] eyes" (Ezek 24:16) would be taken away and that he was not to shed tears or mourn. That evening his wife died.

The next day Ezekiel went about his business as if nothing had happened, and the people asked him why he was acting like this. God told him to say, "Because God is going to take away the delight of your soul—the holy temple" (see Ezek 24:15–23). God himself would defile his own dwelling place (Ezek 24:21), and their sons and daughters would die by the sword (Ezek 24:15–22). They would have no chance to mourn formally and would pine away in their iniquities and mourn with one another (Ezek 24:23). On that day the Babylonian siege of Jerusalem began (Jer 39:1–2; 52:12–30).

Ah, God! Even your gentleness is a fury, a stormy wind and a flooding rain (see Ezek 13:13) which gave Israel over to her idolatrous lovers, who threw down her shrines, broke down her high places, and stoned the people with stones and thrust them through with their swords (see Ezek 16:39–41)!

The corpses of the children of Israel were laid before their idols, and their bones scattered all around their altars (Ezek 6:5). All the great houses in Jerusalem were burned (Jer 52:13), and God "swallowed up all her palaces" (Lam 2:5). Cities were laid waste, high places made desolate, idols and

The Witness of Ezekiel (1)

incense altars cut down (Ezek 6:6). Thousands were led off into captivity to Babylon (2 Kgs 25) and God "cast down from heaven to earth the beauty of Israel" (Lam 2:1).

In vision, Ezekiel had seen a man clothed in linen with an inkhorn by his side. He was told to mark every man and woman on the forehead who sighed and cried over all the abominations that were done in the temple. Then others were told to go throughout the city and kill without pity old and young—men, women, and children—who did not bear the mark (Ezek 9:3–7). Ezekiel had been so overwhelmed by the sight that he fell before God, crying out to him not to destroy everyone (Ezek 9:8–9). God had told him that the iniquity of Israel was exceedingly great, the land was full of bloodshed, and the city perverse, because they say, "The LORD has forsaken the land, and the LORD does not see!" (Ezek 9:9).

God was "crushed by Israel's adulterous heart" (Ezek 6:9), and he was determined "to seize . . . Israel by *their* heart" because they were estranged from him (Ezek 14:5). He sent his "four severe judgments" against them (Ezek 14:21): plague, the terrible arrows of famine, wild beasts to bereave (Ezek 5:17; 14:21), and the sword all around them.

Priests breathed their last in the city (Lam 1:19). Elders sat on the ground in silence (Lam 2:10). Tears ran down the walls of Zion like a river day and night for her children "who fainted from hunger at the heads of every street" (Lam 2:18–19), their lives "poured out in their mothers' bosom" (Lam 2:12). Women of Zion were ravished (Lam 5:11). Princes were hung up by their hands (Lam 5:12). Those left in the city paid for the water they drank, wood for heating came at a price (Lam 5:4), and the people got their bread at the risk of their lives (Lam 5:9). Elders no longer sat at the gate (Lam 5:14), and the music of the young men fell silent (Lam 5:14).

God threw his net over Zedekiah, king of Judah (Ezek 12:13). With his belongings slung over his shoulders he fled with his princes at dusk, escaping through a hole dug out in the city wall. But the Chaldean army pursued. He was overtaken in the plains of Jericho and brought to Babylon (Ezek 12:10–12; Jer 39:1–7).

Then the LORD laid his fury and jealousy to rest. "I will be quiet, and be angry no more" (Ezek 16:42).

"How lonely sits the city that was full of people! How like a widow is she, who was great among the nations! The princess among the provinces has become a slave!" (Lam 1:1). "The kings of the earth, and all the inhabitants of the world, would not have believed that the adversary and the enemy could enter the gates of Jerusalem" (Lam 4:12). "The adversaries saw her and mocked at her downfall" (Lam 1:7). They "clapped their hands" and "shook their heads" (Lam 2:15). "Oh that my head were waters, and my eyes a fountain of tears, that I might weep day and night for the slain of the daughter of my people!" (Jer 9:1). "Is it nothing to you, all you who pass by? Behold and see if there is any sorrow like my sorrow which has been brought on me; which the LORD has inflicted in the day of His fierce anger" (Lam 1:12).

All Is Not as It Seems

So, it is this tragic state of affairs in ancient Israel that leads many Christians to dismiss the salvation of all humankind out of hand. It's impossible, let alone unbiblical, they say. With such severe judgments like this, with all the death and carnage in their wake, the very idea that God will save all is a train wreck. If even God's chosen people went off the rails, what hope can there be for the world's chronic derailments?

But it's the gospel message that God *has consigned all under sin that he might have mercy on all* (Rom 11:32 ESV) and the declaration of God's irrevocable oath that before him all humanity will bow in allegiance (Isa 45:22–24)—*and*, remember, that God will gather together all things in one in Christ, both which are in heaven and which are on earth (Eph 1:10)—that *press us into a corner of conviction*. These divine pronouncements of a good outcome are staring us in the face, even though they're being dismissed by so many Christians who categorically refuse to consider how they might come to pass. Yes, they appear insanely impossible, but we are *compelled* to cling to them on the strength of God's word.

Jeremiah, the prophet who remained in Jerusalem after its destruction, sick to his stomach over all that had happened (remember "the wormwood and the gall"?), feels his strength and hope sinking (Lam 3:18–19). Yet, as faith surfaces from under the weight of horror, he calls to mind the heart of God and draws in a breath of courage: "Through the LORD's mercies we are not consumed. . . . For the LORD will not cast off forever" (Lam 3:22, 31). Mercies? Not consumed? Judgments not forever? What is this? Whistling past the graveyard?

His pen, writing as if with ink dipped in the spilt blood of his people, has just recorded Israel's devastation. What about all those who fell by the sword? What about all those withering away from shortage of bread? What of the little children fainting at the head of every street?

But could it be that the sword, famine, and pestilence Israel suffered (Ezek 6:11) were the very calamities the Romans Letter was referring to hundreds of years later when Paul arrived at the persuasion that because God has given *everything* of himself to us in his Son, therefore no "famine, or nakedness or peril or sword" or any other disaster will "be able to separate us from" his love for us in Christ (see Rom 8:35, 38–39)?

"Then They Shall Know That I Am the LORD"

For there's an intriguing declaration in the book of Ezekiel, repeated over sixty times in its forty-eight chapters. The more we explore it, the more it emerges as massively significant. That declaration states in absolute terms that in the midst of the sin, the turmoil, and the judgments, "they shall know that I am the LORD" (Ezek 7:27). Whether they know him by judgments or mercy, by tenderness or thunder, by fire and brimstone, in strength or weakness, *they shall know him*. Knowing is a beginning, not an end. And the goal of knowing is mercy, that unstoppable determination in God's heart to be known for who he is.

Notice the similarity of thought between what the Romans Letter says is God's end purpose in his judgments and what Ezekiel says is God's end purpose in those judgments. Paul's statement that God "has consigned all to disobedience, that He might have mercy on all" (Rom 11:32 ESV) parallels a declaration with a similar outcome in view in Ezekiel: "According to what they deserve I will judge them; *then they shall know that I am the LORD!*" (Ezek 7:27).

God's goal is that from imprisonment under sin shall flow mercy to all (the Romans Letter). Similarly, in Ezekiel, God's goal is that from judgment of sin shall flow the knowledge of the LORD. Thus, in the two formulations, "knowing that God is the LORD" (Ezekiel) equates with "mercy" (Romans). Notice, too, that the dynamic Paul describes of God "giving them up" to their idols is identical to that in Ezekiel: "I also gave them up" to pagan sacrifices (Ezek 20:25–26). Since, according to the Romans Letter, the outcome of "giving them up" brings humanity to its crisis of human depravity (Rom 1:21—3:18) so that they become positioned for Christ's mercy on all, then we can expect the same intent to be revealed in Ezekiel's book and the other prophets.

In fact, before we move more deeply into Ezekiel, it's advantageous to compare a summary of Paul's thoughts regarding the outcome of the judgments with those of Ezekiel:

Ezekiel: God's "wrath [is] on their whole multitude [Israel]" (Ezek 7:12).
Paul: "Wrath of God is revealed on all the ungodliness . . . of men" (Rom 1:18).

Ezekiel: God "gave them up" to their evil rituals (Ezek 20:25).
Paul: God "gave them up" to the worship of idols (Rom 1:24, 26, 28).

Ezekiel: They worshiped "creeping thing[s], abominable beasts," and idols (Ezek 8:10).
Paul: They worshiped "birds and four-footed animals and creeping things" (Rom 1:23).

Ezekiel: Judgments of famine, wild beasts, pestilence, and the sword (Ezek 5:17; 14:21).
Paul: Tribulation, distress, persecution, famine, or nakedness, or peril, or sword (Rom 8:35).

Ezekiel: By those judgments "you shall know that I am the LORD" (Ezek 5:17; 6:7).
Paul: In those judgments "we are more than conquerors" (Rom 8:37), and they "shall [not] separate us from the love of Christ" (Rom 8:35).

Ezekiel: Result of God's judgments: "They shall know that I am the LORD!" (Ezek 7:27).
Paul: Result of mankind's imprisonment in sin: God has mercy on all (Rom 11:32).

Ezekiel: God provides a sacrifice of atonement, forgiving all Israel (Ezek 16:63).
Paul: God provides a sacrifice of atonement, justifying all mankind (Rom 3:25; 5:18).

Ezekiel: Israel fears their hope is lost and they are cut off. God assures them that he will raise the whole house of Israel from the dead (Ezek 37:11–14).
Paul: Israel fears they are cast away. Paul assures them that it will lead to their acceptance, the reconciling of the world, and "life from the dead" (see Rom 11:11, 15, 26; 5:18).

Ezekiel: God says of Israel, "I am for you" (Ezek 36:9).
Paul: Paul says, "If God is for us," nothing can be against us (Rom 8:31-39).

Ezekiel: "The whole house of Israel" will be redeemed (Ezek 37:11-14; 39:25).
Paul: "All Israel will be saved" (Rom 11:26).

The parallels are remarkable. In both Ezekiel and Paul is the proclamation of the gospel. We see, then, in Ezekiel, the positive outcome of the judgments that Paul saw through the eyes of the gospel.

In Living or Dying, All Come to Know the LORD

The common understanding—more accurately, assumption—among Christians is that it's the ones who survive, who are not destroyed in the judgments—the remnant—who receive mercy and so come to realize that God is the LORD. And naturally this would be the view embraced by those who believe that only some (a remnant) will be saved while most are lost—that judgments involve the saving for, or the loss of, eternal life.

But is this what we find in Ezekiel? In fact, it is not.

First, it's certainly affirmed in Scripture that those who survive on the earth—the remnant—do come to know that God is the LORD, as we see in the following examples:

> They shall eat their bread with anxiety, and drink their water with dread, so that her land may be emptied of all who are in it, because of the violence of all those who dwell in it. Then the cities that are inhabited shall be laid waste, and the land shall become desolate: and you shall know that I am the LORD. (Ezek 12:19-20)

> The slain shall fall in your midst, and you shall know that I am the LORD. (Ezek 6:7)

> Alas, for all the evil abominations of the house of Israel! For they shall fall by the sword, by famine, and by pestilence. He who is far off shall die by the pestilence, he who is near shall fall by the sword, and he who remains and is besieged shall die by the famine. Thus, will I spend My fury upon them. Then you shall know that I am the LORD, when their slain are among their idols all around their altars. (Ezek 6:11-12)

So, in this case those who look on and see their nation's devastation are sobered and refocus their hearts on the awareness that God is their LORD. But to suggest that this group alone comes to know the LORD is a view that falls dismally short of the full outcome of events. Far more is going on than God's dealings with a remnant only.

The startling reality is—and this is the second point—according to Ezekiel's message, *those who do not survive* because of "sword," "famine," and "pestilence" *also come to know that God is the LORD*:

> A disaster, a singular disaster;
> Behold, it has come!
> An end has come....
> Doom has come to you....
> A day of trouble is near....
> Now upon you I will soon pour out My fury,
> And spend My anger upon you;
> I will judge you according to your ways,
> And I will repay you for all your abominations.
> My eye will not spare,
> Nor will I have pity....
> *Then you shall know that I am the LORD who strikes.*
> (Ezek 7:5–9)

> And I will break down the wall that you have smeared with whitewash, and bring it down to the ground, so that its foundation will be laid bare. When it falls, you shall perish in the midst of it, *and you shall know that I am the LORD*. (Ezek 13:14 ESV)

> "You have feared the sword; and I will bring a sword upon you," says the Lord GOD. "And I will bring you out of its midst and deliver you into the hands of strangers, and execute judgments on you. You shall fall by the sword. I will judge you at the border of Israel. *Then you shall know that I am the LORD*." (Ezek 11:8–10)

Here, then, people who are "struck," who "fall by the sword," and "perish," and are "judged," *by these very experiences*, come to know that God is the LORD. Death and perishing, as tragic as they are, are not the end of their story, "for to Him all are living" (Luke 20:38 WEY). Coming to know that "God is the LORD," *that* is the climax of their life and death. For many Christians who have long assumed that death tallies the final score, this idea seems as impossible to grasp as walking on water. Perhaps, they go on to imagine, "they shall know that I am the LORD" doesn't have a redemptive meaning after all. Perhaps, they think, it's a term that describes an awful moment of final, eternal judgment just before death by the sword, pestilence, or famine wipes them out for good. For these Christians "knowing that God is the LORD," then, becomes a drastic act of terminating the wicked, killing them off permanently—period. Or sending them to eternal hell.

But—and third—this interpretation is the most deplorably careless because it ignores massive redemptive issues in Ezekiel that make clear the meaning of "then they shall know that I am the LORD." Certainly, individuals would experience an awareness of God's lordship in progressive stages, but that they *all* finally arrive at the same place—coming to know that God is the LORD in a redemptive way—is clearly revealed in Ezekiel's book.

Dying Is Not the End for All Israel

Couched in one of the most dramatic images in Scripture is a message that death isn't the end for Israel—*not even the end for the ones who have already died in their sins and abominations. Their destiny is, rather, that they will come to know that God is the LORD.* We're all familiar with the vision of the valley of dry bones Ezekiel was given. "Can these bones live?" God asks Ezekiel (Ezek 37:3). A rhetorical question, for sure. God knows what he's about to reveal. Breath will enter the bones, sinews and flesh will come on them (vv. 5–6). A rattling is heard, then bones come together, bone upon bone. Sinews grow, skin covers them, but there's no breath yet (vv. 7–8). Ezekiel is told to prophesy to the breath, "Thus says the Lord GOD, 'Come from the four winds, O breath, and breathe on these slain, that they may live.'" (v. 9). Then follows God's spectacular explanation of this vision:

> Son of man, these bones are *the whole house of Israel*. Behold, they say, "Our bones are dried up, and our hope is lost; we are indeed cut off." Therefore prophesy, and say to them, "Thus says the Lord GOD: 'Behold, I will open your graves and raise you from your graves, O my people. And I will bring you into the land of Israel. *And you shall know that I am the LORD*, when I open your graves, and raise you from your graves, O my people. And I will put my Spirit within you, and you shall live, and I will place you in your own land. *Then you shall know that I am the LORD*.'"
> (Ezek 37:11–14 ESV)

Who are these people? *The whole house of Israel*. And God *does* mean the *whole* house of Israel because he says to Ezekiel that he's going to take the separated tribes and join them together again with Judah so that they are one once more. "I will make them one nation...; they shall no longer be two nations, nor shall they ever be divided into two kingdoms again" (Ezek 37:15–22). So, God is not just talking about a remnant. He's talking about *all* Israel. They're in despair. Their "hope is lost." They feel abandoned—"cut off"—because of their awful sins. Furthermore, it's a vision of the future when they'll all be resurrected. God's commitment towards them doesn't stop. He still calls them "my people," and he's reassuring them that his judgments on them are not the end, despite catastrophes engulfing them like landslides. Through it all, and beyond it all, they'll come to know that God is the LORD when he raises them from the dead and restores the land to them. Apart from being a careless interpretation, therefore, the view that "then they shall know that I am the LORD" is a pronouncement of final, eternal doom is categorically false. *Knowing that God is the LORD reaches beyond death and results in the resurrection of all Israel, and their receiving God's Spirit* (Ezek 37:14).

But the resurrection from the dead traces back to *the one, unsurpassed, pivotal event* that makes it happen.

God's Supreme Act upon Israel That Determines the Destiny of All

The gospel has taught us that there is no resurrection without crucifixion. "If Christ is not risen, your faith is futile; you are still in your sins!" (1 Cor 15:17). Resurrection is an *effect* flowing from a magnificent *cause*. Reasoning backwards, as Paul does in this verse, the fact that all Israel will be raised from the dead means that Christ, their Redeemer, has already risen on their behalf as "the firstfruits" (1 Cor 15:23). Before their resurrection, God had atoned for Israel's sins—taken their judgment upon himself through the death of his Son and so provided forgiveness for them. Thus comes this fascinating imagery in the heart of Ezekiel's book:

God speaks of Israel as a little, abandoned baby, thrown out into the open field (Ezek 16:5), loathed from the day she was born (Ezek 16:5). No one pitied her and washed her clean or wrapped her in little warm covers (see Ezek 16:4–5). Then the LORD passed by and saw her struggling in her own blood. He spoke tenderly to her, "Live!" (Ezek 16:6), and from that day he took her under his care. She grew, matured, and became beautiful, and God made splendid clothing and jewelry for her (Ezek 16:7–13).

The Witness of Ezekiel (1)

Her fame went out among the nations because of all the magnificence God conferred on her (see Ezek 16:14). But it was then that she slid into that fatal independence and began to trust in her beauty and commit harlotry and idolatry with all the nations around (Ezek 16:15–34). God's painful decision to judge pursues her, and he allows all the horrors to come on her that we have already seen (Ezek 16:44–59).

If that were the conclusion of the allegory, the arguments some Christians make for the permanent destruction of most of Israel while leaving a saved remnant only, might hold water. But they're leaking all over the place because they ignore the definitive truth that is the core of Ezekiel's book. And that is the message that *God's judgments are instruments of redemption*:

> "Nevertheless I will remember my covenant with you in the days of your youth.... And I will establish My covenant with you. *Then you shall know that I am the LORD*, [in order] that you may remember and be ashamed, and never open your mouth anymore because of your shame, *when I provide you an atonement for all you have done*," says the Lord GOD. (Ezek 16:60–63)

The atonement. That oceanic event that reverses the tide of human history. That event that sets reality on its head so that because of God's entanglement with it, *grace*, not death, flows out of sin. That event described so clearly in the gospel, shedding its light of power and the passionate love of God on Old Testament judgments. *The sacrificial death of our Savior.* Tread slowly through these verses.

There's one layer of grace loaded on top of another. And one act overturning all acts. God's going to renew his covenant with Israel. It is a covenant that removes all their sins, atoning for all they have done (Ezek 16:63). Such a merciful move will cause them to know that God is the LORD—clearly a *redemptive knowing*—so that, when they see how kindly he deals with them after the judgments, their memory will rise above all the stress of their sins, and, recalling the terrible things they've done, they'll feel ashamed. That shame will come from two directions: first, the recall of their sins; and second, the exposure to God's forgiveness through the atonement he'll make for them, by which he forgives them for all they have done. The three verses above, then, make a few things clear:

(1) This is that tiny, abandoned baby whom God took under his wing—Israel. God's going to forgive Israel—a far-reaching act involving the whole nation. It is, furthermore, an act of forgiving Israel that is absolute—total—covering *the whole house of Israel for all that they have done*. These

very words make necessary an interpretation that encompasses a forgiveness embracing not merely Israel's present at the time of Ezekiel's writing, but the whole history of that nation, which means every man, woman, and child constituting that history—*the history of all that they have done.*

Since it is the "the whole house of Israel" that is to be raised from the dead and receive his Spirit (Ezek 37:11–14), it follows that the whole house of Israel will have been forgiven. How else can it be understood than its inclusion of all Israelites who went into slavery; all who died by the sword, pestilence, and famine; all who languished and remained; all who lived in the past, the then-present, and who live today and will live in the future—men, women, and helpless children of all Israel's generations? The one to whom all things are present hears the lament of his people throughout all time.

(2) This breathtaking forgiveness comes about by means of God "providing an atonement." The word in the original language is the technical one used for the animal sacrifices that prefigured the actual sacrifice of Christ. Undoubtably, here is one of the places where Paul gets his inspiration from in his Romans Letter when he says that because of God's atoning work, Israel's being "cast away"—*yes, cast away!*—will end in their "acceptance" and "life from the dead" (Rom 11:15). "And so all Israel will be saved" (Rom 11:26).

Here in Ezekiel, God speaks of "providing an atonement" as a future event, just as Zechariah's prophecy, some seventy years later, after a remnant of Israel returned from the Babylonian captivity, spoke comprehensively of the time when God "will remove the iniquity of that land in one day" by bringing forth his servant, the Branch (Zech 3:8–9). Clearly, the pronouncements of both Ezekiel and Zechariah speak of the coming atoning work of Christ, the Branch, when God removes all judgment from his people by taking his wrath for sin upon himself through his Son, Jesus, at the cross.

(3) The shame they experience is a redeeming shame. It follows from forgiveness: they will "be ashamed and never open [their] mouth anymore because of [their] shame" (Ezek 16:63). As we have seen, these aren't "the good remnant" merely. They're sinners mortified by memories of "abominations" they committed that made even Sodom look good (Ezek 16:49–52). They've run out of excuses. They're stunned by their sinfulness, speechless when God comes to them with his atoning forgiveness and mercy. Here's a picture daubed in the sharp, blood-red hues of redeeming judgments—judgments that do not simply punish and discipline but lead to shame and redemption.

And we must note that drastic event contributing to the shame:

> I also gave them up to statutes that were not good, and judgments by which they could not live; and I pronounced them unclean because of their ritual gifts, in that they caused all their firstborn to pass through the fire, that I might make them *desolate*, and that they might know that I am the Lord. (Ezek 20:25–26)

We considered earlier the horror of this. Now ponder the psychological trauma following from it.

Desolation Positions Humanity for Grace

Significantly, their wicked behavior leads not to an effect meant to permanently destroy but one meant *to appall them*, and *make them desolate*, so that they might know that God alone is the LORD. As we have learned, because of Israel's suppression of God, and in order to "seize their hearts" (Ezek 14:4–5), he let them go to the lowest point humans can go (imprisoned them!). They experienced the overwhelming distress of pagan "statutes" and "rituals," ones they couldn't possibly live by: sacrificing their firstborn to the fires of the not-gods, Baal and Moloch. Pressured by the terrors of the age, desperate to please their not-gods who hadn't a brain to know what was going on yet who, they think, might help them to survive their enemies, now mindless of the fear of the LORD, their inner voices screaming to turn back, their feet heavy as lead, they step out of their homes with their little ones to go and do the unthinkable.

And the return . . . their hearts too stunned by shock to ache . . . desolation, minds dumbfounded, their houses—once homes—damp with chill terror. And morning after morning, the encroaching stealth of unbearable horror and sorrow.

"That they might know that I am the LORD." The contrast between their pagan life and the ways of Jehovah now thuds through their near-bursting veins as God seizes their hearts by the disasters he let fall on them. Memories haunt, those sweet memories lost: the covenant the LORD had made with them, the joyful festival days they used to look forward to—such happy family and neighborly gatherings—the calm beauty surrounding the temple and the outer court, the sounds of boys and girls playing in the streets (see Zech 8:5), the strains of the songs of David wafting through the land, the sunrise as they go forth to their labor until the evening (see

Ps 104:22-23). Now, shame floods their soul at the stinging contradictions of pagan effigies: pain, misery, childless homes, futility. Reality stabbing deep that "they [had] sacrificed their sons and daughters to demons" (Ps 106:37). Excruciating awareness of knowing God *by what he was not*. Self-loathing because of the evils they'd committed (see Ezek 20:42-44). Hearts melting, hands feeble, spirits faint, knees feeling weak as water (Ezek 21:7). And minds only just managing to give insanity the slip, clinging to the cold comfort that God's judgments at least showed he cared about what they did. "What you have in mind shall never be," he'd said (Ezek 20:32).

Not then, after all, abandoned. Utterly melted, yes. Poured out like molten metal in the smelting furnace (Ezek 22:18-22), their sacred images reduced to slag at their feet. "So you shall be melted . . . , *and you shall know that I am the LORD*; I have poured out my wrath upon you" (Ezek 22:22 ESV). "O Israel, you are destroyed, *but your help is from Me*. I will be your King; where is any other?" (Hos 13:9-10).

A Disturbing Mercy

Even now, then, in the dwindling light, when human escape routes have reached their end and the air hangs laden with grief and despair, comes a dramatic turn. Out of the depths, God knows that despondency of soul is a voiceless prayer to the unknown God (see Rom 8:26), and it is he, the one, true God, who is determined to be known. Paul surely had his nation in mind when he put it so stunningly: "When we were *enemies* we were reconciled to God through the death of His Son" (Rom 5:10). God's response sends shock waves around the world. His passionate concern that Israel might know that he is the LORD—through judgements of deportation, of the sword, famine, and pestilence—now rises to its heights, not the depths of hell or annihilation, as feared, but the heights of mercy and restoration. Now they are about to know that God is the LORD *by what he is, not only by what he is not*. "I am for you, and I will turn to you" (Ezek 36:9).

> "Now I will bring back the captives of Jacob, and *have mercy on the whole house of Israel*; . . . after they have borne their shame. . . . When I have brought them back from the peoples . . . , and I am hallowed in them in the sight of many nations, then they shall know that I am the LORD their God. . . . And I will not hide My face from them anymore; for I shall have poured out My Spirit on the house of Israel," say the Lord GOD. (Ezek 39:25-29)

Astonishingly, God's going to bring "the whole house of Israel" back into their own land, cleanse them from all the filth of their idols, take the heart of stone out of them, and give them a new heart. He'll put his Spirit within them and cause them to walk in his ways, and they shall be his people and he will be their God, and they shall dwell in the land (see Ezek 36:24–30). Here is the glorious God of Israel: "*For the LORD will not cast off forever.* Though He causes grief, yet He will show compassion according to the multitude of His mercies. For He does not afflict willingly, nor grieve the children of men" (Lam 3:31–33).

Even more intriguing is the *reason* God gives for restoring Israel. Hearing the news of Israel's downfall, the nations were saying, "These are the LORD'S people, and yet they had to leave his land" (Ezek 36:20 NIV). The nations' interpretation of things is a profound concern to God because he cares about them. *He wants them to view things aright.* And for this reason,

> I had concern for *my holy name*, which the house of Israel had profaned among the nations wherever they went. Therefore say to the house of Israel, "Thus says the Lord GOD: 'I do not do this [restore Israel, put My Spirit in them and cleanse them] for your sake, O house of Israel, *but for My holy name's sake*, which you have profaned among the nations wherever you went. And *I will sanctify My great name* which has been profaned among the nations, which you have profaned in their midst; *and the nations shall know that I am the LORD* . . . *when I am hallowed in you before their eyes.*" (Ezek 36:21–23)

God Acts for the Sake of His Redeeming Name

In these words, the meaning of God's desire that people come to know that he is the LORD is placed beyond dispute. Three verses, and God's concern that the nations should know his *redemptive* name is mentioned four times. His name has been besmirched by Israel's behavior. In God's self-interest for his name and the preservation of it lies the salvation of Israel and the nations. "*All flesh* shall know that I, the LORD, am your Savior and your Redeemer, the Mighty One of Jacob" (Isa 49:26). God's holy name is precisely identified with his care for Israel, and through them to the nations, with his power to redeem and protect and with the keeping of his promises to all his creation by means of judgments that lead to mercy and restoration.

God restores the whole house of Israel because "*I will be jealous for My holy name*" (Ezek 39:25).

In God's protectiveness of his name is the protection of Israel and the nations—*humanity!* As humanity trusts in what God's name proclaims about himself and what he does for Israel and the nations, there, in that trust, is their salvation. To know who he is is to be saved by who he is. He is not like powerless, pagan gods that are not-gods and cannot save. He is Almighty. And "he delights in mercy" (Mic 7:18). The word "LORD" in the declaration "then they shall know that I am the LORD," in the original language is *Yahweh* (Jehovah). This name is used when God is referring to his *relationship* with his people. He's the only God, the Creator, the Father and Redeemer and sustainer of his creation, the keeper of his covenant and promises.

Thus, when he makes that vow that before him every knee shall bow, he declares it with the ringing tones of, "Look to Me, and be saved, *all you ends of the earth!*" (Isa 45:22). His desire—which will accomplish what he pleases (Isa 55:11)—is to be known in this redemptive way, even through his judgments. When Jesus referred to "knowing" God, he equated such knowledge with the essence of being: "This is eternal life," he said, "that they may *know You*, the only true God, and Jesus Christ whom You have sent" (John 17:3). Knowing God is life in its eternal existence. From the words alone, then, the declaration that "they shall know that I am the LORD" belongs to things eternal, affirming God's desire that "the nations may know Me" as he redeems them (Ezek 38:16).

The Silence of History

Yet, once again, faith slams headlong into *what seems to be* reality. No such wholesale restoration of Israel is described in the history books. It's as if it disappeared down a historical sink hole. The unvarnished fact is, however, it never happened. Alternative interpretations abound among those whose theological framework doesn't allow for the salvation of all, and who believe that everyone's eternal destiny is settled before death or at the second coming of Christ. They conclude that the restoration of the whole house of Israel is not to be taken literally. It means *the whole of them that are saved*, they contend. So, they attempt to squeeze a limited restoration of Israel into a time slot prior to the second advent of Christ and assume that is the restoration of a sort of "whole house of Israel."

The Witness of Ezekiel (1)

For anyone taking the Bible seriously, such interpretations are embarrassing attempts to dive in at the shallow end. It's plainly obvious that a restoration of a few at the climax of human history isn't what Ezekiel saw in his prophetic mind. Too many far-reaching events described in Ezekiel, chapters 36 to 39, categorically do not fit into a this-side-of-history happening.

There has to be another explanation . . .

[Before we continue, two points need to be noted here. First, the Old Testament gives full recognition to a remnant returning from captivity and being blessed by God: "For the seed shall be prosperous, the vine shall give its fruit, the ground shall give her increase, and the heavens shall give their dew—I will cause the remnant of this people to possess all these" (Zech 8:12). But theologians and Christian teachers have tended to emphasize that it is only that remnant that will be saved, principally, I think, to support the reality of what they see: a small number of Jewish people returning to their land or accepting Christ throughout the ages. But it is obvious that they are attempting to square their theology with the facts on the ground. The totality of the wording of the promises, however, will simply not allow this interpretation. Nor can the drama describing their fulfillment support the idea of the salvation of only a few. God's declarations speak repeatedly of all Israel—the whole of it—being restored (Ezek 37:1–14; 39:25).

Second, some have taken the fallback position that the promises are conditional upon Israel's faithfulness. And since Israel failed to come up to the bar, they were rejected and replaced by individual believers in the Christian church—"spiritual Israel"—in whom the promises will be fulfilled. But though the Romans Letter teaches that all believers are included in Israel as Abraham's seed (Rom 9:8), the belief that Israel was rejected and has been replaced by Christians, as "spiritual Israel," is a huge theological error. Such a view does violence to the most basic meanings of language. It makes the overall motif of Scripture unintelligible. And it flouts the meaning of the promises and the unbreakable oath God made. It, furthermore, makes it impossible to believe in God's salvation of all. Putting it simply, this flawed interpretation appears to be merely a neatly packaged way of asserting that God starts his redemption all over again, having failed in the first attempt. Both Ezekiel and the Romans Letter clearly show that God will save all literal Israel. And that he will do so is proof positive that, by extension, he can and will save all the world. We shall explore this further in volume 2 of this book.]

Chapter 7
The Witness of Ezekiel (2)
The Saving of All Israel Mirrors
the Saving of All Humanity

"THE WHOLE HOUSE OF Israel" is a definitive phrase, if words are to mean anything at all. And, as we have seen, the whole house of Israel includes those who have committed abominations and who also feel that hope is lost and they are cut off—as well as the separated tribes. Furthermore, as we shall also see, the restoration involves a *return of all Israel to faith in God, and belief in Jesus Christ their Redeemer*. Since, then, such a wholesale spiritual renewal and restoration of that nation has not happened in history, what other explanation is open to us?

Sounds of Eternity

When we finally relent and conclude that alternative interpretations have run themselves into the ground, a moment of startling realization hits us like a bolt from the blue: the biblical data we've explored in Ezekiel's book portrays the restoration of all Israel not in *historical time*, but, remarkably, in the scenes of the *final judgment*, when, as we saw in the introduction to this book, every knee shall bow and every tongue shall take an oath that in Christ alone is their righteousness and strength—the time that Peter might be referring to as "the restoration of all things" (Acts 3:21) and Paul, as "the dispensation of the fullness of the times" (Eph 1:10).

This should not be surprising. Though it is, considering our natural bent for fence-sitting when it comes to our fear of believing that God really

The Witness of Ezekiel (2)

can and will save everybody. After all, it *has* to be this way, doesn't it? Yes, of course. That simple word of Paul's now makes sense: "*All* the promises of God in Him [Jesus Christ] are Yes, and in Him Amen" (2 Cor 1:20). And what is Jesus for us? He himself said, "I am the *resurrection* and the *life*" (John 11:25). He is the second Adam, the one who spearheads the resurrected humanity when he commences the new creation in his kingdom (Rev 21). "As in Adam all die, even so in Christ all shall be made alive" (1 Cor 15:22). We have already seen that when every knee bows and every tongue confesses allegiance to God, it will happen in the final judgment (Rom 14:10–11) before God's throne upon which stands a Lamb as though it had been slain (Rev 5:6). Then God has "mercy on all" (Rom 11:32).

Thus, one of the major reasons for the lack of belief in the salvation of all is *the placing of the events surrounding Israel's restoration on the wrong side of history.* Like the Jewish leaders in Christ's day—and the disciples of Jesus, too, at first—we have been mistakenly looking for a *natural*, physical, this-side-of history restoration of Israel.

The fact is, the ultimate fulfillment of the promises of God to Israel—and by extension, to the world—is a *supernatural thing*. It involves the new creation, a kingdom "cut out without hands," as Daniel puts it (Dan 2:45), when "this mortal must put on immortality" (1 Cor 15:53). It must come to us *from* Jesus' resurrection *through to* our resurrection. This is, surely, why Jesus said to those two disciples as they walked to Emmaus village, "*Ought not* the Christ to have suffered these things and to enter into His glory?" (Luke 24:26). Dare we say it? Yes, he *ought to have suffered.*

If Jesus had such longing to open the way for us—and he did—it was necessary for him to tragically suffer. He is the door to the resurrected world, blazing the trail through sorrow and death that he might gift mankind with life after all its grievous sin and dying. This world of death cannot produce it. "The world is passing away along with its desires" (1 John 2:17 ESV). It was said, remember, of those great men and women of faith mentioned in the book of Hebrews that "all these, though commended through their faith, *did not receive what was promised*, since *God had provided something better for us*" (Heb 11:39–40 ESV). They did not receive the promise? Yes, because God had a far greater plan than a mere renovation of this earth. That "something better" is the kingdom of God.

The temporary, happy restorations that Israel has so far seen in this world are only reassuring hints in time of what resurrection life will be in eternity. *They must not be confused for the real thing.* Only with an eternal perspective can all the promises be seen to be a total *yes* for us. Be surprised no more. Ezekiel's prophecies of restoration look to the time *after* this earth's history is done.

So first, Ezekiel speaks in historical time when catastrophes as judgments came upon his people, *then his mind leaps into events in the coming kingdom where the promised restoration is fulfilled in its totality.* This prophetic process—from time to eternity—is revealed in passages in Ezekiel's book when the light of the gospel shines on them. Then we see that Ezekiel is telling of future heavenly events, not future earthly ones. The evidence for this is clear.

Speaking on the timeline of human history, Ezekiel communicates God's jealousy burning against the nations who gave Israel's land to themselves as a possession out of pure spite (Ezek 36:5), and he vows they will bear their shame (Ezek 36:7). Meanwhile, God promises that Israel shall shoot forth its branches and yield its fruit (Ezek 36:8–12).

Then comes that leap in Ezekiel's prophetic mind. Out of protectiveness for his name, God is going to "sanctify," or "set apart," his name before the nations by resurrecting Israel (Ezek 37), taking them from the nations, having "mercy on the whole house of Israel" (Ezek 39:25), bringing them into their own land, cleansing them from their filth, giving them a new heart, pouring out his Spirit on the whole house of Israel after they will have borne their shame (Ezek 36:22–38), and causing them to walk in his ways and dwell in the land which will be made to look like the garden of Eden (see Ezek 36:23–35; 34:29). There, God will be their God and they shall be his people as he sets his dwelling place in their midst forevermore (Ezek 37:28). This is not the language of earth.

It's the language of the coming kingdom, a vision of a new creation, when all Israel, raised from the dead, is in its immortal, incorruptible state and God lives with them forevermore (compare Ezek 37:11–14 with 1 Cor 15:53 and Rev 21:3).

Further evidence for this comes in the next scenes of Ezekiel's visions:

"After many days," in "the latter years," "Gog" in the land of "Magog" will come against "those brought back from the sword" (Israel!) to attack them (Ezek 38:11–16).

Then follows this:

As the nations' long-standing hatred for God's chosen one, Jesus the Messiah, and his people comes to a head, the nations of the world move against the people of God. God's fury rises (see Ezek 38:18) and all humanity ("all men who are on the face of the earth") shake at his presence (Ezek 38:20). There's an earthquake (Ezek 38:19). Mountains are thrown down (Ezek 38:20). The LORD Almighty brings Gog into judgment with pestilence and bloodshed, flooding rain, great hailstones, and fire and brimstone (see Ezek 38:22). *And then all nations come to know that God is the LORD* (Ezek 38:16; 39:7). To people familiar with the Bible these events are immediately recognizable.

They are events described in the book of Revelation. And there we gain some understanding of when, approximately, they happen: *as one of the climactic events of the final judgment* when all nations in coalition—Gog and Magog, "which are in the four corners of the earth" (Rev 20:8)—surround the resurrected people of God to attack them, and fire comes down from heaven and devours them (Rev 20:7–10). At this time all stand before God in the final judgment. Those written in the Book of Life are in the city. The rest go into confrontation with God described as the lake of fire (Rev 20:15). Finally, as we have seen (Rom 14:10–11), every knee bows and every tongue confesses that in God alone is their righteousness and strength.

Ezekiel, most likely, would not have realized the expansiveness of the vision given him. He, like all the other prophets, prophesied in part and saw only in part (1 Cor 13:9). It's the gospel that indicates what side of history these events belong to.

So, then, we know when the events occur: in the final judgment. And we know their outcome: that Israel and the nations come to know that God is their LORD (Ezek 38:16; 39:7). In the following pages I will attempt to suggest a sequence, staying within the parameters of the data given in Scripture. I will also put together some of the spiritual and psychological dynamics that are inferred from the biblical drama as it unfolds. This suggestive sequence builds on the issues implied in the texts and the redemptive goal they are clearly leading towards.

Scenes of the Final Judgment

The final judgment is no placid courtroom scene. High drama is being played out on the world stage—the confrontation between good and evil where the ultimate, naked anger of an infuriated world against God reaches boiling point. Presumably, at this time "the whole house of Israel" is resurrected in the "general resurrection" of all mankind. We must assume that God displays before Israel the glory he has produced in the lives of believers in Christ "who proclaim the praises of Him who called [them] out of darkness into His marvelous light" (1 Pet 2:9). Thus, the meaning of a seemingly mild comment in the Romans Letter takes on huge proportions:

> But through their fall, to provoke them to jealousy, salvation has come to the Gentiles. (Rom 11:11)

God, having brought Israel to an end of themselves ("their fall"), now uses an emerging, jealous longing in them to have what has already come to the gentile believers through faith in their Savior, Jesus—salvation, safety, joy within the city of God. Through the unlikely motive of jealousy, God is positioning Israel for that same faith in his loving mercy through his Son, their Messiah.

He pours "the Spirit of grace and supplication" on them. Before their eyes is presented a view of the throne of God with a "Lamb as though it has been slain" in the midst of it (Rev 5:6). All Israel, in deep shame, "will look on Me whom they pierced" (Zech 12:10)—*that gentle Lamb, their Messiah, Jesus, the Christ*—and, coupled with stark views of their historical and personal idolatry, mixed with a terror of being left without God, side by side with his intoxicating mercy shown to others through the sacrifice of his Son for them, *they mourn.*

"Yes, they will mourn for Him as one mourns for his only son, and grieve for Him as one grieves for a firstborn" (Zech 12:10). Here, in the slain Lamb, God's beloved Son, is the forgiveness God has provided from deep within his yearning heart "for all they have done" (Ezek 16:63). Now, consciously aware of their poverty of soul and abandoning their long-held resistance towards their Messiah, they are ready for faith. The Spirit gifts them with precious trust in Christ. God cleanses them, giving them a new heart and a new spirit, taking away their heart of stone (see Ezek 36:25–27).

Somewhere in here their mortality puts on immortality (Ezek 37) like all those in Christ before them, and they, along with all believers in Christ throughout the ages, are caused to "shoot forth [their] branches and yield [their] fruit" (Ezek 36:8) as God sets his dwelling place among them (Ezek 37:26–27). Thus, God "sanctifies" and "hallows" his name in them, showing it to be pure and a thing of glorious beauty through a restored Israel in the sight of all nations. All the sorrows and sufferings of Israel are now swallowed up in joy. And "the nations shall know that I am the LORD . . . when I am hallowed in you [Israel] before their eyes" (Ezek 36:23). The nations see the character of God, how he loves, rescues, nurtures, defends, and glorifies. But so far, they want none of it.

The Nations Revolt

God is still the object of their contempt. Where was he when they needed him? Why so much unfair suffering which he could have prevented? What about all the injustice that has left the majority of the world's inhabitants objects of failed hopes and misery? Something further must happen to move them to know him. Ezekiel refers to "spiteful minds" (Ezek 36:5). Global, internal pain seeks an object to revile. They have found it: Israel, and her perceived vulnerability (Ezek 36:2–3). In those spiteful minds an unimaginable, universal rage is about to burst forth like masses of ripened boils. What was that anger of the older son in the parable all about again?

His young brother has returned home after running riot in far off places. His father throws a party for him (Luke 15:25–32) and the older brother is beside himself with jealousy and resentment. The Jewish leaders knew Jesus was talking about them. Through his parables Jesus often purposely needles people to get them to know the state of their own minds. Now it's the nations' turn to be jealous. Yet, the Lord is fully aware of the intimacies of every heart. He knows that humanity's festering rage is but a disguised wail of unimaginable grief and loss. And he alone can heal it. The trouble is, having suppressed God, and under the delusion of their idols, they're not aware of the true cause of their anguish. Now Almighty God is in their face. Now resistance to him is raw. Now God deliberately reveals "before their eyes" (Ezek 36:23) his merciful lovingkindness towards all believers and the whole house of Israel. Like a red rag before a bull, it enrages the narcissism of the nations.

Purposeful provocation is going on here. Their Redeemer must use strange means to break through their rigid unbelief.

At the sight of those rescued from all humanity who "shine forth like the sun in the kingdom of their Father" (Matt 13:43), the world's wrath breaks out without reserve. Unlike Israel's reaction, their jealousy takes a sinister turn—a vicious drive to destroy those who have received God's mercy while they themselves appear to be neglected and left out. Jealousy, often the playground of children and immature lovers, is, in the final judgment of the nations, about to become the destructive force of the world.

Madness has moved in. Reason has taken its leave. Recall yet again that mankind's will is not free.

The pervasive and persistent suppression of God has led to global inability to see the true issues. Spiritual disorder of the mind has taken over. Without faith in God there is no human spirit to guide the twists and turns of the heart. Irrational emotions dominate, steering humanity headlong towards the ultimate clash with reality. But humanity's schemes do not thwart the redemptive plans of Almighty God.

Human Rebellion Corralled and Directed

Rather, it is God's sovereign, loving might that thwarts human schemes by his interplay with their evil to abort what would otherwise be their own self-destruction on steroids. To understand this is a major ingredient of belief in God's ability to pull all the world back from the brink. As we have seen in the Romans Letter, the nations have been given over to the bondage of their idolatrous alternatives to God. They are "imprisoned" in lunacy and, as Ezekiel reveals, trapped in a rage against the one, true God who appears to obstruct their personal and global egotism (see Ezek 38:10–13). Now the LORD says of Gog and Magog, "I will turn you around, put hooks into your jaws, and lead you out, with all your [armies]" (Ezek 38:4) and "You will come into the land of those brought back from the sword [Israel]" (Ezek 38:8). Here, through the prophet, God intends to show that the coming events are *his* initiative—all designed to reveal his redemptive power to a world whose masses are in the death grip of God-resistance.

God will now use humanity's despair of *him* and its alternative, delusional, godlike confidence in *itself* and "hedge it up" and "wall it in" (see Hos 2:6) to make himself known to them. Remember that God's sovereignty is not about controlling the human will regardless of humanity's wishes, but about revealing that the will, without him, has no controls and therefore no power to direct its wishes. It is now subject to the whims of passions without purpose.

His sovereign action, therefore, in the final judgment, of "giving them over" to their rage against him and his people is the act of releasing mankind's mob mindset to play out its pandemonium, a mankind that has lost the self-mastery even to say, "Not so, Lord! How could we do such a thing?!" Astonishingly, therefore, the final judgment involves *a God-baiting attack upon himself*. As bizarre as this may sound, ponder this: it is not the first time.

Divinely Guided Showdown

"Jesus, *delivered up according to the definite plan and foreknowledge of God*, you crucified and killed by the hands of lawless men" (Acts 2:23 ESV). The opposers of Jesus played right into God's hands precisely because God delivered himself first into *their* hands. To get his enemies to yield to his goodness, Jesus, first, had to yield to their badness. The hatred the enemies of Jesus had for him was exactly what led to the death of the Son of Man for the purpose of saving those enemies.

While the "definite plan" to give his Son for humanity's sin was God's, it was, providentially, wicked men, no longer in control of themselves, who did the odious job for him. The human act of murdering the Son of God, therefore, was also the divine act of sacrificing God's Son for the sin of the world. Thus, "the wrath of men shall praise [him]" (Ps 76:10). And now, just as "the Prince of life" (Acts 3:15) gave himself to enemies who were hammering in the nails, similar dynamics to that drama are about to be fulfilled in the saga of the final judgment as their Creator-Redeemer allows the nations to march against him.

So it is that in this final judgment the Lord presses in from all sides mankind's God-hate and self-perceived god-status and channels it towards *the ultimate showdown between God and his creation*, which is designed climactically to bring "mercy on all" (Rom 11:32). Even in the destabilizing recklessness of a cosmic clash between the forces of good and evil, the purpose of the Lord does not change. In fact, it *is* his purpose. "*I* will send a fire on Magog.... *Then they shall know that I am the LORD*" (Ezek 39:6). It is as if God were saying, "When they attack me, then they shall know who I am, their Creator-Redeemer and Father." Hence the final battle—mankind's supreme march of folly.

Mankind's Final Attack

"Why do the nations rage, and the people plot a vain thing? The kings of the earth set themselves, and the rulers take counsel together, *against the LORD and against His Anointed*, saying, 'Let us break Their bonds in pieces and cast away Their cords from us'" (Ps 2:1–3). "A mighty army" storms in, "covering the land like a cloud" (Ezek 38:9, 15–16). Their number "as the sand of the sea" (Rev 20:8), they surround "the camp of the saints and the beloved city" (Rev 20:9). "I will bring you against My land," the LORD says, "*so that the nations may know Me, when I am hallowed in you*, O Gog, before their eyes" (Ezek 38:16).

God shows his fury in his face (Ezek 38:18). "All the earth" is about to be "devoured with the fire of [his] jealousy" (Zeph 3:8). Boggling the mind even further, now comes the revelation of *God's* jealousy.

First in the final judgment came Israel's jealousy towards the saved gentiles. *Then* comes the nations' jealousy towards saved Israel. *Now* God's jealousy towards his creation is revealed. Clearly, God has no intention of letting it be lost on the nations in that day that the emotion of jealousy driving their rage against *him* is the very emotion he has towards *them*. Just as God, this side of human history, took humanity upon himself to make himself known through his Son, so in the final judgment, to make himself known, God reveals an emotion deep within him that the nations are altogether too familiar with. "For in My jealousy and in the fire of my wrath I have spoken" (Ezek 38:19). "You shall worship no other god, for the LORD, *whose name is Jealous*, is a jealous God" (Exod 34:14).

As the world seethes with jealousy over their sense of not being treated as special, like Israel has been, so God's jealousy seethes over not being treated as special, the only one, before whom all other gods are not-gods. And just as the world seethes with jealousy over their sense of missing out on the blessing God is giving to Israel, but not, seemingly, to the nations, so God's jealousy seethes over missing out on the devotion humanity is giving to their not-gods rather than to him—to *him* who sustains all creation, moment by moment, who loves the world of his creatures in poignant intimacy (see Ps 139), and who spends all that is precious to him redeeming them. Thus, as he did to Israel in former days, he sets his case before all nations.

The Final Judgment: God's Controversy with the Nations

"They have no knowledge who carry about their wooden idols, and keep on praying to a god that cannot save. Declare and present your case" (Isa 45:20–21 ESV). "Have I been a wilderness to Israel, or a land of thick darkness? Why then do my people say, 'We are free, we will come no more to you'?" (Jer 2:31 ESV). "What fault did your fathers find in Me that they strayed so far from Me? They followed worthless idols, and became worthless themselves" (Jer 2:5 BSB). "What more," he asks, "could have been done to My vineyard that I have not done in it?" (Isa 5:4). But God's questions—rhetorical replies to unspoken complaints—imply that mankind has an issue with God also. Where were you? Why all this suffering? Why did you let it all happen? Why didn't you stop it?

Pause: God's very questions suggest creative intent. As we have seen, God's dealings with Israel are a microcosm of how he relates to the world. Why, then, would he pose these issues before the nations, and why would his jealous love be presented as a major issue in the final judgment, if it were not for the fact that, though the world hates him, he intends to persuade it and win it back to his lordship through his judgments, and not to let most of it perish in hell or be annihilated? Ironically, the world's hope for itself lies in the very thing it resists: God's jealous love, which is heaven-bent on tearing his world away from its destroyer. For God is *arguing* with humanity.

He is *persuading* them. He has "a controversy with the nations; He will plead his case with all flesh" (Jer 25:31). The very dynamic of the final judgment starts with a violent controversy (the nations' attack on the city of God) and moves to climactic persuasion (God's jealousy and human jealousy). And you can be sure God wins the argument.

The reason "every knee" bows in allegiance (see Isa 45:22–24) is that they will have been persuaded, not forced. His jealous love for the world's devotion—his irresistible intention that they might know him—is hardly solved by a near-universal and eternal wipeout of the human race. Divine jealousy's specific endgame is to recapture the love and devotion of a world that has jilted him—*by their coming to an intimate knowing that he is the LORD*. As we have seen, this does not deny that God's reaction to the world includes permitting *consequences* as *judgments* to go their full length, even to death. But just as Israel went under the sword yet were resurrected and, in the process, came to know that God is the LORD, so also with the world.

Thus, God's loving wrath rises, a jealousy like fire licking up everything in its path (see Ezek 38:18–23). What happens next is beyond the perimeters of present reality to comprehend. But what Scripture gives us is this: that day will be so overwhelming that at the appearance of the face of God utter cataclysm ensues. "Earth and heaven fled away. And there was found no place for them" (Rev 20:11), and "all men who are on the face of the earth shake at [his] presence" (Ezek 38:20).

It is as the armies of Gog and Magog surround "the beloved city" (Rev 20:9) that the glory of God's consuming jealousy appears. Like the burning blue of sapphire and the golden yellow of amber, God's radiance fills the world (see Ps 72:19; Isa 6:3) and moves humanity to a mind-devouring guilt and shame. Before its magnificence, mankind's jealousy appears as it is: the outflowing of disfiguring pride; a trifling yet cruel, deadly, endlessly violent, unforgiving expression of the world's broken heart foisted on all the families of the earth (see Rom 1:30–31). What is clear, certainly, is that the revelation of God's pure love leads to the revelation of mankind's evil. God's jealousy is a jealousy of eternal, passionate love, spurned. Theirs, a jealousy of endless hate, frustrated. Extreme human jealousy would destroy the one it cannot have. God's jealousy, extreme with love, wins back the one previously denied him.

In the presence of this unexpected, sublime mystery of God's heart, the armies of Gog and Magog attempt to cover the shame of their empty souls. Blame becomes their mask—that convenient way of deflecting their true state. And, thus, in a display of worldwide mayhem, they turn on one another. In global frenzy, "every man's sword [turns] against his brother" (Ezek 38:21). Each step is the unfolding of humanity's lethal descent into madness without its loving Creator and Redeemer who holds the worlds in his hands (see Col 1:17).

Humanity's Internal Conflict in the Presence of God

And yet, as their self-destructiveness rages on, in the recesses of their minds the conflict between wanting what the believers have yet hating them for having it tears at them as they see, as through "a wall of fire" (Zech 2:5), "the whole house of Israel"—gentiles and Jews—"a peaceful people, who dwell safely" (Ezek 38:11). Desire and revolt devour their minds. Why would they want what they hate? They are melting in the turmoil—hearts aching while limbs thrash about destroying everyone around them. And pressing in hard pursuit is the love of the eternal God, jilted.

Facing him, their brokenness becomes a searing reality. A growing longing for him becomes a terrifying need. All the more bewildering to them now is how they could possibly have lived so long separated from him without perishing under its weight. The fire of his glory, before which the sun is ashamed (see Isa 24:23), now makes clear the lunacy of their suppression, as if, like children covering their eyes, they'd repeated day after day, "You can't see me!" Yet, arrayed before him, he is a stranger to them (Matt 7:23).

It is a pitiful grief that the one in whose presence is "fullness of joy" (Ps 16:11) should appear like a ravaging lion in their eyes (see Hos 13:7–8). Now, like Israel who went through the same experience before them, their minds are in the terror of outer darkness even while exposed to the unyielding brightness of his Being. There is a gnashing of teeth (Matt 8:12). Like Isaiah when he saw the LORD (Isa 6:1–5), the nations are undone, unclean, their narcissism falling off like flakes of gray, making bare the dead souls beneath. Paralyzed with awe, an unfamiliar longing tugs against a death wish for the rocks to fall on them to hide the shame of what is now clear to them: the denial of their Creator-Redeemer (see Rev 6:12–17).

A heart-cry, foreign to their ears, for the unknown Father weakens their limbs as they attempt to steel themselves against the majestic possessiveness. Still awash with surges of irrational hate for the saved people of God but pulled toward an opposing current of longing to be among them, harboring even still vain attempts to squelch the frantic voice within, like men drunk out of their minds, they push on aimlessly striking at all within their reach. The strain is too much; the grief, too haunting. Nothing holds. Collapse is imminent. Weapons drop from their hands (Ezek 39:3). "Flight perishes from the swift" (see Amos 2:14). Their spirits exhausted, they come to an end of themselves. Gog and Magog fall upon the mountains of Israel (Ezek 39:4).

Nothing is left of human pride. "In that day a man will cast away his idols of silver and his idols of gold, which they made, each for himself to worship, to the moles and bats" (Isa 2:20). "The LORD alone will be exalted in that day, but the idols He shall utterly abolish . . . when He arises to shake the earth mightily" (Isa 2:17–19).

The Death of the World

This staggering global cacophony of final judgment God describes through the prophet Ezekiel as his *pestilence, bloodshed, floods, hailstones,* and *fire and brimstone raining down* (Ezek 38:22).

And it is also a description of a final judgment that for many Christians is the final straw. If they'd had even a shred of hope that salvation for all might be possible, for them the final judgment rips it up. The world's nations—Gog and Magog at the four corners of the earth—*are, after all, judged and dead*. Their chance is gone. It's too late, they presume. They suffer eternal exclusion.

Judgment Leads to Reconciliation

But striding across time is the one man for all humanity whose life and death and resurrection on behalf of earth's race makes it clear that this interpretation has come about because Christendom has turned a blind eye to many of the far-reaching implications of Christ's death on the cross.

Adam brought the condemnation of death to all peoples, but this one man brings the vindication of life to all (Rom 5:18). Through this man, God's Son, the Son of Man, God took the world's judgment for all time upon himself (Heb 10:12). Through him God has, therefore, reconciled himself to the world (2 Cor 5:19) and become its defender. And now, *through these precise cataclysmic acts of the final judgment*, he is reconciling the world to himself (2 Cor 5:19). Hence, as we have seen, the final judgment cannot be a repeat of the judgment God took upon himself in Christ but is rather *a compelling, persuasive dynamic leading mankind towards that reconciliation* (2 Cor 5:20)—towards that "mercy on all" (Rom 11:32).

Redemptive judgments—that's what these judgments are all about, designed to position violent humanity for that impossible act of divine, gentle mercy. These massive realities stand behind God's intentions in the final judgment described by Ezekiel. There, dead or not, God specifically says that *he led this divinely directed chaos of confrontation to reveal himself to all nations* (Ezek 38:16).

> In the judgment God brings the nations against Israel *so that the nations may know him* (see Ezek 38:16).
>
> In the judgment God glorifies his name in Israel *so that the nations might know him* (see Ezek 36:23).
>
> In the judgment God sends a fire in Magog *so that they might know him* (see Ezek 39:6).
>
> In the judgment God glorifies himself in Gog *so that the nations might know him* (see Ezek 38:16).

Christian theology's fatal attraction with death gouges out the core of Ezekiel's message (Ezek 16:60–63) and leaves it to shrivel up on the margins of the page. We saw earlier in this chapter that God's astonishing declaration of atonement—a prefigurement of Christ's sacrificial death on the cross (see Zech 3:9) to bring forgiveness and resurrection to the whole house of Israel—*is also the hope of the world*. It is precisely what God does for Israel—forgiving all of them for all that they have done and bringing them to life eternal through Christ—that prefigures the whole of humanity's destiny. For Israel is a mirror image of the world, a witness to what the Creator-Redeemer does for all mankind in light of what he did for all Israel through the sacrifice of the Messiah (compare Zech 3:9 and John 1:29).

And what shall we say of the witness of the prophet Zephaniah, writing from Jerusalem fifty years earlier than Ezekiel? He describes the final judgment day's intense drama of divine, jealous love and its awesome resolution in one of the most far-reaching and breathtaking passages in the Bible:

> "Therefore wait for Me," says the LORD,
> "Until the day I rise up for plunder;
> My determination is to gather the nations
> To My assembly of kingdoms,
> To pour on them My indignation,
> All My fierce anger;
> All the earth shall be devoured
> With the fire of My jealousy.
> *For then I will restore to the peoples a pure language,*
> *That they all may call on the name of the LORD,*
> *To serve Him with one accord."*
> (Zeph 3:8–9)

Spectacular in its scope, Zephaniah's declaration from the LORD reveals *his all-encompassing intention to restore the whole human race to devotion to him.* Words come nowhere near to approaching its magnificence. Just as God says of Egypt that he will "strike down Egypt, *healing as He strikes*" (Isa 19:22 NEB), so here also Zephaniah declares that in the final judgment, God's jealous love will devour this idolatrous world, while at the same time *healing* it—restoring it so that *everyone will call on his name in total agreement*—with one accord ("shoulder to shoulder"; NASB). What Zephaniah saw confirms the interpretation of Ezekiel's final judgment scene laid out in this chapter. A summary of Zephaniah's words looks like this:

1. It is the final judgment scene—the revelation of God's jealousy before all kingdoms.
2. It is argument, controversy: God's indignation, jealousy, and the nations' shame.
3. It implies that God's argument prevails: the earth is devoured by it.
4. There is resolution: the world is transformed, speaking faith and devotion to God.

Fire and Brimstone: The End or the Process?

It's with the understanding that the nations come to know that God is the LORD, and that God will restore to the peoples a pure language after being "devoured" by God's jealousy, that we get a clearer view of the expression, "fire and brimstone."

> I will bring him [the nations of Gog] to judgment with pestilence and bloodshed; I will rain down on him, on his troops, and on the many peoples who are with him flooding rain; great hailstones, *fire and brimstone*. (Ezek 38:22)

Debate has swirled around whether these terms are literal or figurative. But that misses the point. The question is, rather, what is the term "fire and brimstone" describing, and what does it accomplish? What is the intent of what's being said with this term?

Does fire and brimstone describe the *end* or the *process*—the *termination of events* or the *unfolding of them*? Is fire and brimstone what happens when all assessments of right and wrong are settled and duly appointed judgments are pronounced, followed by execution? Is that the fire and brimstone—the execution itself? Or is the pandemonium, the turmoil, the clash of wills, minds finally faced with blazingly shocking reality, the crushing realization of human sin, the melting revelation of God's glory, and the utterly overwhelming relief and joy over God's mercy that brings restoration—*is that the fire and brimstone?*

A careful reading of Ezekiel chapters 38 and 39 makes it evident that pestilence, hail, floods, and "fire and brimstone" is language used to describe the convulsing process of God's total, persuasive unveiling of himself to the world, and mankind's traumatic collapse in the face of it—a preparatory state for their merciful redemption, whether dead or alive.

Taking the reference to fire and brimstone as a *terminating of the issues* of the final judgment rather than a *description of the drama as it is being played out* misses the essence of the final judgment. Obviously, if God is revealing his consuming, fiery jealousy to the world, he wants to be heard (see Ezek 36:6; 38:18–19; Zeph 3:8). And certainly, if the nations are moving in to attack him and the city, they think they have a cause, no matter how delusional (Ezek 36:5; 38:11–12). The idea that God is simply going to exterminate them by fire and brimstone can hardly be considered the way to settle God's issues and those of humanity.

The Witness of Ezekiel (2)

The final judgment involves God and the nations stating their grievances (Ps 50). His jealousy over their idolatry has to be made clear. Their jealousy over God's seeming favoritism has to be brought into the light. The reasonableness of God's jealousy has to be explained, and how it revolts against the nations' obsession with soul-destroying idols. They must discover how God has baited them by revealing his mercy to others. God has to reveal how their resistance to him is wrapped up in a suppressed longing for him, which is why he baited them in the first place. They must be shown how the folly of their idolatries has led to self-inflicted ruin, and that God's actions of giving them over to the results of their suppression of him were not an abandonment but acts of loving wrath against evil, which brought them to an end of themselves to prepare them for trust in him (Rom 1:24, 26, 28).

There is a devastation and torment in the presence of so much glory and lost opportunity that brings a keenly painful longing for the kingdom of God as the only place of safety and peace. And beyond this—the Lamb, whose eyes are like seven eyes sent out into all the earth (Rev 5:6), peers into the empty souls of every man and woman with the tantalizing warmth of life and love waiting to be welcomed.

All these issues and more are ablaze in the engulfing language of fire and brimstone which becomes *the expression of the cataclysmic revealing of the glory of God to the world.* Clearly, there are more layers to coming to "know that God is the LORD" than meets the eye, far more than the raining down of burning sulfur could ever resolve. But the complexity of "knowing" could certainly be described as fire and brimstone.

Ever since the days of Abraham when Sodom and Gomorrah were destroyed by literal burning rocks and sulfur, the term "fire and brimstone" and other severe atmospheric conditions have been used figuratively by the prophets to describe God's confrontation with mankind.

When, for example, on this side of history, God declares his judgment on Assyria, he speaks of "His tongue like a devouring fire" (Isa 30:27) and the breath of the LORD "like a stream of brimstone" (v. 33).

And notice that Asaph, the head of music in King David's court, contrary to what at first appears to our minds, is focused not on the frighteningly destructive forces of nature *but on the redemptive outcome they are meant to bring about:*

> O my God, make them like whirling dust,
>   like chaff before the wind.
> As fire consumes the forest,
>   as the flame sets the mountains ablaze,

> so may you pursue them with your tempest
>   and terrify them with your hurricane!
> Fill their faces with shame,
>   *that they may seek your name, O LORD.*
> Let them be put to shame and dismayed forever;
>   let them perish in disgrace,
> *that they may know that you alone,*
>   *whose name is the LORD,*
> *are the Most High over all the earth.*
> (Ps 83:13–18 ESV)

At first read, these verses pull us up sharp as images of dust storms, forest fires, tempests, and hurricanes flash across our minds. But their essence is not the storms and fires, whether they are literal or figurative. Asaph wants his enemies to become *so ashamed* that they might "seek God's name" and come to realize that *Jehovah alone is the Most High who is sovereign over all.* So how does Asaph want them to come to this conclusion? He uses language describing nature's ability to bring *crisis and cataclysm*, language depicting circumstances so beyond the control of his enemies that they become "dismayed forever" and are spoken of as even "perish[ing] in disgrace." *But clearly their eternal doom is not what Asaph means by this language.* He's imploring God to overwhelm them in ways that will make himself known to them. Then, permanently—"forever"—they'll be humbled and know that Jehovah alone is Most High over all the earth.

In other words, the storm, the fires, and the tempests and hurricanes are not a description of the end of the enemies but a description of the *process* God uses to bring his enemies to know him as LORD of all.

And then, think of the drama of God's deliverance of King David from Saul and his enemies. David describes the event in terrifying imagery: the earth shaking and trembling (Ps 18:7); God descending with smoke coming out of his nostrils, his mouth like a fiery blowtorch (v. 8); the channels of the sea and the foundations of the world being uncovered (v. 15). Obviously, these descriptions are figurative, but, again, the issue doesn't lie there. What David was doing was describing his victory over his enemies and Saul as *an entirely supernatural event*, attributing power to God totally beyond human reach and viewing himself as the helpless, grateful recipient of unparalleled mercy. And the whole redeeming process is described in convulsive terms of fire and earthquakes.

But, as we have seen, fire and brimstone is not only a description of physical battles, it is also an intense picture of the divine argument of the truth of the Creator-Redeemer in the presence of the outrage of idolatry.

The instances in Scripture of God and Jesus arguing with the nations and with individuals of the world are so prolific—from Genesis through to the Psalms, from the prophets to Jesus and Paul—that it would takes pages of this book merely to list them. What they make clear is that God's persistent salvation dynamic is *persuasion*, the persuasion of love in all forms: *argument, judgments, vengeance, glory, loss, grace, mercy*. Persuasion does not, of course, save a person. What it does is to break down all their defenses, leaving them stunned by the absurdity of their stance, and thereby to position them for the redemption of faith in God's mercy through his Savior. And the irresistible strength of God's arguments lies in this: his word will not return to him void; it will accomplish all that he pleases (see Isa 55:11). His word is like a fire and like a hammer that breaks even rocks in pieces (see Jer 23:29).

This dynamic is diametrically opposed to eliminating most of his creation. If the nations are to come to a knowledge of God, they must be utterly overwhelmed with the reality of truth so that "the nations may know" him. If they were to die by annihilation or the suffering of an eternal hell, then that would abort the process of God's persistent persuasion involving all the issues that the final judgment has brought to the fore.

It's the view that "fire and brimstone" is the end of the argument rather than a description of the stirring process of winning mankind over that makes it difficult for so many Christians to see the obvious when it comes to God's irrevocable, unbreakable oath and the response of every human being—"every knee" and "every tongue"—making a vow of allegiance to their Creator-Redeemer.

For they reckon there are two groups mentioned by Isaiah (Isa 45:22–25): those who bow willingly, and those who are angry with God and are forced to bow as their last act before being wiped out by literal, all-consuming fire. They *have* to see it this way because they started off with a false premise: that the fire and brimstone is an act of force that shuts down all further dispute.

With this mindset, how else can they interpret the shame the masses of humanity feel in the final judgment than as an angry bowing down by forced submission before the fires lay them waste? *This is religious cynicism at its worst.*

Who in the world has *not* been angry with God at one time or another, or all the time in the majority of cases? Faith in God's redeeming love is the act of humbly laying down that anger and trusting him through the confusion. As we have previously seen it's because the nations come to know that God is the LORD in all his love and mercy that they feel shame, and *all, having received mercy*, bow the knee in allegiance to him, acknowledging that their own goodness and power have been a sham all along, and God alone, in his Savior, Jesus Christ, is the only righteousness and strength there is.

Thus, we need to note again that they do so because the persuasive fire-like and brimstone-like revelation of God, and of their broken humanity, plus the merciful love that still, nevertheless, pursues them, leads them to shame over their unjustified anger towards him. In this way, they are positioned for faith.

So, cataclysm is the total clash of the minds and hearts of mankind with the mind and heart of God. "Fire and brimstone" is the full-on, undiluted, dramatic, and finally resolved dispute between God and the nations, designed to reveal his rescuing love for his creation.

Scripture does not pull any punches about the results of this. Such a head-on clash involves the collapse of the human race and what appears to be the death of the world. We have already referred to the prophecy in Zephaniah in regard to God's restoration of all humanity. But it shouldn't go unnoticed that in that same book just two chapters earlier, Zephaniah boldly proclaims that "in the fire of his jealousy, all the earth shall be consumed; for a full and sudden end he will make of all the inhabitants of the earth" (Zeph 1:18 ESV). *So, wrath and fire, and the earth being consumed—and a "full end"—are not, in fact, the end of the story.*

God's breath of jealousy which consumes is that same breath that brings restored life to the world. Read his words again, because faith needs bolstering when judgments are all around: "'Therefore wait for Me,' says the LORD, 'until the day I rise up for plunder; My determination is to gather the nations to My assembly of kingdoms, to pour on them My indignation, all My fierce anger; all the earth shall be devoured with the fire of My jealousy. For then *I will restore to the peoples* a pure language, that they *all* may call on the name of the LORD, to serve Him with *one accord*.'" (Zeph 3:8–9).

Just as Israel comes through death in the final judgment because of the atonement for all their sins and the resurrection that follows through the life of the risen Christ, so also it is for the nations. It is impossible to conceive that the nations come to know God as the LORD without *having their sins atoned for and without their consequent resurrection to immortality*. The link between what happens to Israel in the final judgment and what happens to the nations is Jesus Christ.

He who gave his life for Israel (Ezek 16:60–63) gave that same life of his for the world (John 1:29). He who was raised to life for the sake of all Israel (Ezek 37:1–14) was raised to life for the sake of the whole world (1 Cor 15:22). Consequently, as *all Israel* is redeemed in the final judgment, so also is *all humanity* (Rom 14:10–11; 11:26, 32).

So, is it after their death that the nations come to know that God is their LORD, or at their resurrection?

The Justification of Life for All Mankind

We are told simply that they shall know that God is the LORD. Whether this knowing is before or after their resurrection is not made clear. But it is all the same to God for *all souls belong to him*, dead or alive (see Ezek 18:4) since "to Him all are alive" (Luke 20:38 NIV). "No one dies to himself" (Rom 14:7). "Whether we live or die we are the Lord's" (Rom 14:8). It was for this reason that Christ died, "that He might be the Lord of both the dead and the living" (Rom 14:9). Just as Israel, the witnesses to the world, are described as going through death to come to know that God is the LORD, so also the world goes through its death as part of the process of coming to know that God is the LORD.

In the scenes of the final judgment, when the nations fall, they are getting closer to that positioning for faith. All that was precious to them has come crashing down. It was necessary in the final judgment for them to be witnesses of their walls falling in. Idolatry's scientific sophistications, its global god-status, its decimating wars, its slave-master cruelty, its human-centered religions, its accomplishments of social evolution and economic development, its so-called spiritual transcendence, its endless round of pleasures, have brought the world only ruin and demonstrated to all that happy human existence without God is impossible.

The nations now go through that same sense of futility that Israel went through at its downfall. A cry of despair rises up before God. "As a woman with child about to give birth writhes and cries out in pain, so were we in Your presence, O LORD. We were with child; we writhed in pain; but we gave birth to wind. *We have given no salvation to the earth, nor brought any life into the world*" (Isa 26:17–18 BSB). Humanity's dreams have failed to fulfill humanity's destiny. "Unless the LORD builds the house, they labor in vain who build it" (Ps 127:1).

But he "who inhabits eternity, whose name is Holy," who "dwell[s] in the high and holy place," also dwells "with him who has a contrite and humble spirit, to revive the spirit of the humble, and to revive the heart of the contrite ones. For [he] *will not contend forever*, nor will [he] *always be angry*; for the spirit would fail before [him] and the souls which [he has] made" (Isa 57:15–16).

God knows the heart of the world as if it were the heart of a single human being. He deals with the nations as he would deal with a solitary soul. He sees the oppression of humanity, as he saw Israel's oppression under the Egyptians in that history long ago (Exod 3:7). He hears the cry of each person under their taskmasters: "For I know their sorrows" (Exod 3:7). He's fully aware that his creation groans with the pains of childbirth (Rom 8:22), and their afflictions are his afflictions (see Isa 63:9). He bears mankind's griefs and carries their sorrows (Isa 53:4). He knows that the world has a broken heart, and each of its shattered pieces is lodged in the soul of every human being, alive and dead.

In reply to the nations' despair, our gentle God brings to them encouraging words:

> Your dead will live; their bodies will rise.
> Awake and sing, you who dwell in the dust!
> For your dew is like the dew of the morning,
> and the earth will bring forth her dead.
> (Isa 26:19 BSB)

Then, as the LORD did with Israel, he now does to the nations. He points them to his beloved Son "in the midst of the throne . . . a Lamb as though it had been slain" (Rev 5:6). The Lord teaches the nations what the sacrifice of Jesus, his Son, means; how the Father and the Son gave their life for the world to bring them back to his heart; how in the Son's sacrificial life and death, as they trust in him by his Spirit, they are taken up into his righteousness; and how they live in the strength of his life for them.

The world now recognizes that light that had been attempting to push its way into their blind souls was the eye of Jesus sent out into all the earth (Rev 5:6). The world will be amazed that what had never been told them before, they will see with their own eyes, and what they had never heard

The Witness of Ezekiel (2)

of, they will be forced to consider (see Isa 52:15). They will be shocked that "the stone which the builders rejected has become the chief cornerstone" (Luke 20:17). And humanity will mourn, as they also, like Israel, "look on [him] whom they pierced" (Zech 12:10). Through the atoning sacrifice God made for them as well as for Israel, God places upon them a spirit of supplication. They realize they've been fighting viciously against the Lord of life, the Savior and defender of the world. They see now that in hating God they have been loving their own death (see Prov 8:36).

Now, through the mercy of God their mourning is about to turn to gladness.

The nations—having nothing left of themselves, overwhelmed by the thought of their lifelong suppression of their Creator-Redeemer, seeing for the first time that God, the Lion, is actually a gentle Lamb sacrificing himself for them—now crushed and full of shame, are open to the gift of faith in Jesus, their Savior. God's mercy comes to them, and, through the Spirit, they are given the power to believe in all that the Lord has done for them, and the robe of his righteousness is given them.

Then, like the sound of trumpets on a festival day, comes God's dramatic announcement, the climax of all humanity's hopes and history. Significantly, from the place where death came to the nations is the place where life will come to them, just as the place where humanity slaughtered the Prince of life became also the place of their redemption:

> In this mountain
> The LORD of hosts . . .
> . . . will destroy . . .
> The surface of the covering cast over all people,
> And the veil that is spread over all nations.
> He will swallow up death forever.
> (Isa 25:6–8)

The covering of death that was choking *all people and all nations everywhere* is itself about to be choked. The moment has come when that heavy veil that hangs over all people, living and dead, is lifted by the strong arm of the life-giving Redeemer, and the eyes of all finally look up into eternal light. "I will *ransom them from the power of the grave*; I will *redeem them from death*. O Death, I will be your plagues! O Grave, I will be your destruction!" (Hos 13:14). Only faith in God's promises can allow us to comprehend this. Human reason simply cannot face its jarring oddity.

And so, as the people of God, on pins and needles of awe, stretch their gaze to see what is happening beyond the emerald walls of the city, the dead of all ages, young and old, babes in arms, youth in all their strength, the forgotten, the unburied, the rich, the poor, the wailing victims of horrible injustice and an aborted life, accompanied by hosts of angels, rise from their graves like newly greened grass on an eternal spring day. Death is robbed of its victims. Death perishes from inactivity. Death dies. "O Death, where is your sting? O Hades, where is your victory?" (1 Cor 15:55).

What is it to destroy death's veil from all people and all nations—to swallow up death forever? Death is a negative state of "no-life." For it to be swallowed up means that something gloriously positive has displaced it, pushing it out of its space, filling the empty, dark vacuum—the universal triumph of Jesus Christ's resurrected life. *And if that covering of death is to be removed from all people, if that veil of death spread over all nations is to be swallowed whole, then it means that Christ's death and resurrection is going to be effective for the whole world—past, present, and future.*

The message is not that Christ will give life to some and not others. Rather, life takes over, thereby annulling death. All people who ever lived, all nations throughout the history of the world, are released from its power—delivered by resurrection. They no longer experience death. In that day, death will not reside in some places and be terminated in others. *Death itself becomes nonexistent.* "There shall be no more death" (Rev 21:4). That *cannot* mean "there shall be no more death *from this point on*"—the point, that is, of the final judgment—for that would mean prior to that point, death would still reign over billions of people who are dead *up to the point*. Or, to put it another way, "no more death" would apply only to those limited few who are saved. But it would still exist and reign over those who are lost—lost by annihilation or hell. If that were so, then it would mean that death still exists, persistent in its prisonlike grip on the masses that had died before the divine pronouncement of eternal life for the few who are redeemed.

No, when Scripture says death will be swallowed up and removed from all nations and all people (Isa 25:6–8), it is not talking about some people living who will never die anymore, while most people in the process of dying will remain dead when they die. The pronouncement is not about people who live and people who die. *It is a pronouncement about death itself.* It is death that is finished. Nor is Scripture talking merely about a worldwide redemption from death—a process of being brought back from it (see Hos 13:14). There is a destruction of death itself—the end of that order of not-existence. Death in essence will be swallowed up in life—the life of Christ for all mankind.

If death, in those eternal times were still to hold billions of lost still in its grip, then Christ's atonement, which counts all mankind justified in his life (Rom 5:18), would not be true but a cruel lie. Nor would it be true that God "will wipe away every tear from their eyes," nor would it be true that there will be no more sorrow (Rev 21:4), for if death were still to reign over the loved ones of the saved, then grief's tears and sorrow would remain for those loved ones lost. But when God wipes away all tears from their eyes, he does so, not by creating an amnesia of the redeemed, but by destroying the source from which those tears spring—the loss of loved ones in death. No longer will those lost be separated from those who long cherished them. They will be redeemed from death and united once again by ties never more to be broken.

God's plan to "gather together in one all things in Christ [who is life!] both which are in heaven and which are on earth—in Him" (Eph 1:10) explicitly involves the universal annulment of death's power to separate. *Death's separating power will be displaced by eternal life's reconciling power.* Were just one person to remain dead, or in the death grip of hell, death's power to separate would still hold sway in the universe, and Jesus Christ's resurrected life could not be said to *reign*. For death to be destroyed—swallowed up—means that nobody, anywhere on the globe and at any time in the history of the world, is dead anymore and separated from loved ones. Death is a *sting* (1 Cor 15:55). Its cruel blade will be ripped out by the strength of Jesus' eternal hand—every man and woman, boy and girl snatched from its penetration, delivered from its power, and finally gathered together in one in Jesus Christ.

When *all people, all nations* have the blanket of death lifted from them, graves everywhere spring open, and all humanity in various stages rises to glorious immortality, and the earth once again buzzes with joyful, tireless life from hamlet, to village, to town and city throughout all nations of the earth. Resurrected now, search where you would on that day, you will find no remnants of dead bones or crumbling graves—no place somewhere where a living death of hell burns. "The earth shall cast out the dead" (Isa 26:19). What, then, is death's mission on that day? It has none. It has nothing more to do. It is given the pink slip. It is fired from its duty. It, itself, starves to death from no human beings to consume. It ceases to exist. But it dies not merely from nonuse.

Death is *judged*. Death, that violent assault on the image of God in humanity, receives the execution of annulment. It is not enough to say that it disappears. For the original death was not a mere misfortune. It was a judgment against humanity's suppression of God (Rom 5:17–18). But now, through "the man for all humanity," Jesus Christ (Rom 5:18), humanity is declared innocent and *death* is judged, and therefore it, itself, must be condemned and executed, never having the authority anymore to bring any soul to the judgment of the end of its life. For God, through his Son, has judged in favor of mankind (Rom 5:18; 8:19–22). He is its defender, and therefore death is pronounced unjust and unjustified.

Thus, Adam's kingdom of sin and death is finally eliminated from the earth. "As in Adam all die, even so in Christ all shall be made alive" (1 Cor 15:22). The reason death is swallowed up is that Christ's kingdom of life has pronounced judgment on Adam's kingdom of sin and death. All rise from their graves because Christ's resurrection on their behalf has justified them (Rom 4:25). Eternal life reigns through the second Adam, the resurrected Christ, the man for all men and women. In the final judgment, because all are raised for eternity, no one bows in fear anymore to the not-god of death.

The Festival of Joy for All Creation

Now, we see God himself preparing the nations for a universal festival of gladness for all people. On the mountains of Israel, where Jesus the lifegiver destroys death forever, the LORD makes a feast for all people, a feast of wines and choice foods (see Isa 25:6). The whole world erupts with joy. The poor find that the wealth of God's kingdom is theirs. The thirsty, drunk on mercy, thirst no more. Wide-eyed, the hungry are blessed and filled. There, the sorrowful burst with laughter (see Luke 6:20–21), and the lame man leaps and runs to the rhythms of the everlasting morning. The one who is mute sings at last with the sky lark, and sickness flees away in the wholeness of new bodies that love to whirl in the dance. Endless gladness rests in the heart of every soul.

Deeply tender moments follow as loved ones and friends meet again, and enemies, now reconciled, have their tears wiped away "from all faces" (Isa 25:8). The disgrace and reproach God's believing people have suffered throughout the millennia are removed from all the earth (Isa 25:8). And hearts swell with so much gratitude that they cry out, "Behold, this is our God; we have waited for Him; we will rejoice and be glad in His salvation"

(Isa 25:9). This "waiting for Him" has been the heart-cry not only of Israel but also of all humanity, even though, like that soul-ache at the sight of a beautiful sunset on the sea's horizon, they did not know what that yearning was. But now the whole creation knows at last the meaning of its long-felt, inexplicable longing to be reborn to eternity (see Rom 8:22).

The final judgment, then, far from splitting the world in two, sending some to the kingdom of heaven and expelling some to hell, *is its glorious and universal reconciliation*, "the restoration of all things" (Acts 3:21) "by Him" who "reconcile[s] *all things* to Himself, by Him [Christ] whether things on earth or things in heaven, *having made peace through the blood of His cross*" (Col 1:20). In the final judgment, the witness of all believers throughout the ages will have done its work on the nations: the gentiles to the Jews, the Jews to the nations of the world, for in the judgment God "gather[s] together in one all things in Christ, *both which are in heaven and which are on earth*" (Eph 1:10). Thus, humanity experiences the convulsive yet life-giving wonderment of the bringing together of all its broken parts. Once we allow our minds to open to this *impossibly real reality*, we see that there is no contradiction between God's irrevocable, unbreakable oath that every knee shall bow to him and the descriptions of the final judgment in the book of Revelation. Suddenly, then, biblical texts, previously skimmed over unnoticed, come tumbling from their pages:

> All nations whom You have made
> Shall come and worship before You.
> (Ps 86:9)

> All the ends of the earth shall see
> The salvation of our God.
> (Isa 52:10)

> All nations shall come and worship before You. (Rev 15:4)

> One act of righteousness [Christ's] leads to justification and life for all men. (Rom 5:18 ESV)

> The whole creation groans and labors with birth pangs. (Rom 8:22)

> He will gather together in one all things in Christ, both which are in heaven and which are on earth. (Eph 1:10)

It pleased the Father . . . by Him to reconcile all things to Himself . . . whether things on earth, or things in heaven. (Col 1:19–20)

So at the name of Jesus every knee will bow, of those who are in heaven and on earth and under the earth and that every tongue will confess that Jesus Christ is Lord, to the glory of God the Father. (Phil 2:10–11 NASB)

As in Adam all die, even so in Christ all shall be made alive. . . . He [will] put all enemies under His feet. (1 Cor 15:22, 25)

He will destroy . . .
. . . the veil that is spread over all nations.
He will swallow up death forever.
(Isa 25:7–8)

All the earth shall worship You. (Ps 66:4)

All the ends of the earth shall fear Him. (Ps 67:7)

Arise, O God, judge the earth;
For You shall inherit all nations.
(Ps 82:8)

He shall speak peace to the nations;
His dominion shall be from sea to sea.
(Zech 9:10)

The nations shall fear the name of the LORD,
And all the kings of the earth Your glory. . . .
When the peoples are gathered together,
And the kingdoms, to serve the LORD.
(Ps 102:15, 22)

I will also give You as a light to the Gentiles,
That You should be My salvation to the ends of the earth.
(Isa 49:6)

We trust in the living God, who is the Savior of all men, especially of those who believe. (1 Tim 4:10)

For God has consigned all to disobedience, that he may have mercy on all. (Rom 11:32 ESV)

The Witness of Ezekiel (2)

Every creature, now vindicated in the final judgment through the sacrifice of Christ on their behalf, dwells safely. "All the ends of the world" (Ps 22:27) have returned to the LORD. Peace and joy are theirs in the embracing arms of God, their Father. Idolatry is forever renounced. The one, true God and his Savior is worshiped and adored, and, with free will fully restored to humanity, God's unbreakable oath now returns to him, fulfilled in his creation as "every knee" bows and "every tongue"—even all those who were previously angry at him—swears an oath in overwhelming gratitude and joy that in Christ alone shall be their righteousness and strength (see Isa 45:22–24; Phil 2:10–11).

A Preview of Volume 2

WHAT DOES THE GOSPEL mean by *election*? Will only *a few* be elected for salvation? Does Jesus really speak about hell? At Christ's second coming, isn't the world going to be divided into *sheep and goats*? What does the book of Revelation have to say about *the lake of fire*?

These issues and more are explored in volume 2 of *God's Unbreakable Oath*.

Volume 2 demonstrates clearly from Paul's Letter to the Romans that God's election is his act of predetermining salvation for all mankind, not just a few.

We see Jesus saving those who received him. But what was he doing for those who rejected him? Wider contexts are investigated that reveal the mystery of how God works to save the hardened. With these contexts we return to our focus on Jesus. We discover *purposeful* provocation of his enemies to bring salvation to them, either here or in the final judgment when their resistance breaks down. This section examines Jesus' references to "hell" and "everlasting punishment."

Volume 2 also explores the Biblical data on the reconciliation of all things in heaven "through the blood of the cross."

Revelation, Ezekiel, and Paul show that the purpose of the "showdown" between God and humanity during the attack on the city of God in the final judgment is to reveal his redemptive glory. We learn what John means in his book of Revelation by the term "fire and brimstone." We discover how "torment" can be experienced in the presence of the Lamb and yet how the Lamb relieves it. We explore the soul-crisis of unbelievers that leads to the supreme struggle with God and his glorious mercy for them all. And we note that the nations, after they have gone through "the lake of fire," bring their glory into the city of God. Finally, we contemplate the joyful reconciliation of all God's creation.

Index

Genesis
17	89
3:6	84
3:15	81
3:21	77
6:5–6	25
12:2–3	87, 88
12:3	99
12:6	89
12:7	88
12:10	89
12:11–20	89
13:1–4	89
13:14–15	89
13:16	89
15:1	89
15:2–3	89
15:5	89
15:6	89
15:8	89
16:1–4	89
17:5	87
17:17	90
17:18	89
21:5–6	90
22:13	52

Exodus
3:7	140
29:38–44	54
34:6	81
34:14	128

1 Kings
8:58	61

2 Kings
25	2, 105
17:5–8	2
17:16–23	2
17:24–33	2
19:17–18	2
19:25	2
24:8—25:21	2

Psalms
36	104
50	135
139	128
2:1–3	127
8:1	43
14:1	84
14:2–3	19
16:11	15, 131
18:7	136
18:8	136
18:15	136
22:27	81, 147
23:3	92
33:11	5
33:13–15	93
36:9	15, 103
45:2–4	53
51:17	83

Psalms (cont.)

65:2	43, 75
65:5	43, 75
65:8	75
65:9	24
65:11	24
66:3–4	5, 43
66:4	146
67:7	146
72:19	129
73:11	84
76:10	127
82:8	62, 146
83:13–18	136
83:16	4
86:8–10	43
86:9	145
102:15	146
102:22	146
103:13	24
104:5	24
104:22–23	116
104:24	24
106:20	16
106:37	116
115:4–5	102
115:8	102
121:3–4	99
127:1	140
139:11–12	84
145:9	24

Proverbs

8:36	25, 104, 141
20:24	74
21:1	74

Ecclesiastes

5:16	92
9:5	41

Isaiah

2:11	92
2:17–19	131
2:17	49
2:19–21	49
2:20	131
5:4	128
6:1–5	131
6:3	129
6:5	81
11:9	6
16:5	34
19:22	133
24:23	130
25:6–8	141, 142
25:6	144
25:7–8	146
25:8	144
25:9	145
26:12	74
26:17–18	140
26:19	140, 143
27:6	101
30:27	24, 135
30:33	135
37:20	101
40:22	61
42:3	53
42:7	53
43:10–13	98
43:10–11	2
44:8	104
45:6–7	2
45:12	3
45:14	3
45:15–17	2
45:15	4
45:18	3, 4
45:20–21	128
45:21	3, 17, 36
45:22–25	137
45:22–24	2, 34, 43, 106, 129, 147
45:22	3, 4, 77, 118
45:23–24	46, 75, 95
46:9–10	3
49:6	99, 146
49:15	24
49:26	117
52:10	36, 145
52:15	27, 141
53:1	31
53:3	31

Index

53:4-6	28
53:4	30, 140
53:5-6	57
53:5	54
53:10	32
53:11	32
55:11	5, 118, 137
57:15-16	140
57:15	19, 101
57:16	83
60:1	53
60:3	99
61:1-3	24
61:1-2	53
61:2	53
61:3	53
63:9	78, 140

Jeremiah

2:5	24, 83, 128
2:13	57, 104
2:19	104
2:31	128
3:17	99
7:30	101
7:31	102
7:32	103
9:1	106
10:23	74
11:13	101
19:4	102
23:29	137
25:31	129
32:27	75
39:1-7	105
39:1-2	104
52:12-30	104
52:13	104

Lamentations

1:1	105
1:7	106
1:12	106
1:19	105
2:1	105
2:5	104
2:10	105
2:12	105
2:15	106
2:18-19	105
3:18-19	106
3:22	106
3:31-33	117
3:31	106
4:12	106
5:4	105
5:9	105
5:11	105
5:12	105
5:14	105

Ezekiel

36—39	119
37	122, 124
38—39	134
5:5	101
5:6	101
5:17	105, 108
6:5	104
6:6	105
6:7	108, 109
6:9	25, 105
6:11-12	109
6:11	107
7:5-9	110
7:12	108
7:27	107, 108
8:10	101, 108
8:11-12	101
8:12	101
8:14	101
8:16	101
8:17	102
9:3-7	105
9:8-9	105
9:9	105
11:8-10	110
12:10-12	105
12:13	105
12:19-20	109
13:13	104
13:14	110
13:20-23	102
14:4-5	115

Index

Ezekiel (*cont.*)

Reference	Pages
14:5	105
14:21	105, 108
16:4–5	112
16:5	112
16:6	112
16:7–13	112
16:14	113
16:15–34	113
16:16	101
16:17	101
16:20–21	103
16:26–30	102
16:31	101
16:36	103
16:39–41	104
16:42	105
16:44–59	113
16:49–52	114
16:60–63	100, 113, 132, 139
16:62–63	4
16:63	100, 108, 113, 114, 124
18:4	5, 139
20:25–26	107, 115
20:25	108
20:26	103
20:31	103
20:32	102, 116
20:42–44	116
21:7	116
22:6	102
22:7	102
22:9	102
22:11–12	102
22:11	102
22:12	102
22:18–22	116
22:22	116
22:27	102
22:29	102
23:37	103
23:39	103
24:15–23	104
24:15–22	104
24:16	104
24:21	104
24:23	104
33:25	102
33:26	102
34:29	122
36:2–3	125
36:5	122, 125, 134
36:6	134
36:7	122
36:8–12	122
36:8	124
36:9	109, 116
36:20	117
36:21–23	117
36:22–38	100, 122
36:23–35	122
36:23	124, 125, 132
36:24–30	117
36:25–27	124
37:1–14	119, 139
37:3	111
37:5–6	111
37:7–14	91
37:7–8	111
37:9	111
37:11–14	100, 108, 109, 111, 114, 122
37:14	112
37:15–22	112
37:26–27	124
37:28	122
38:4	126
38:8	126
38:9	127
38:10–13	126
38:11–16	122
38:11–12	134
38:11	130
38:15–16	127
38:16	118, 123, 128, 132
38:18–23	129
38:18–19	134
38:18	122, 128
38:19	123, 128
38:20	123, 129
38:21	130
38:22	123, 131, 134
39:3	131
39:4	131
39:6	127, 132

Index

39:7	123
39:25–29	116
39:25	100, 109, 118, 119, 122

Daniel
2:45	121

Hosea
2:6	126
2:19–20	24
9:7	101
11:3	85
11:8–9	27
13:7–8	131
13:8	25
13:9–10	116
13:9	25
13:14	141, 143
14:8	92

Amos
1:9	25
1:11–15	25
2:14	131

Micah
7:18	32, 81, 118

Habakkuk
1:8	104
1:9	102

Zephaniah
1:18	138
3:8–9	133, 138
3:8	128, 134

Zechariah
2:5	130
3:8–9	114
3:9	32, 99, 132, 133
8:5	115
8:12	119

9:10	146
12:10	124, 141

Matthew
5:3	85
7:23	130
8:12	131
11:28–30	24
11:29	25
13:9	86
13:43	125
16:16–17	73
19:14	24
19:26	18, 20
23:37	26
27:46	28

Mark
1:15	86
3:5	26
14:33	28
14:34	28

Luke
2:32	99
5:8	81
6:20–21	144
7:50	86
12:12	92
15:21–22	93
15:25–32	125
19:10	57
20:17	141
20:38	110, 139
22:43	28
23:34	57
24:26	121

John
2	26
1:1–2	27
1:4	24
1:9	24
1:11	31
1:14	27

John (cont.)

1:29	32, 53, 97, 99, 133, 139
3:16	23, 64, 97, 98
3:18	86
3:27	73
4:22	98
6:37	72
6:39	73
6:44	73
6:63	91
6:65	73
10:30	28
11:25	121
11:33	26
11:39	91
11:43	91
12:31–32	60
12:32–33	33
12:32	96
14:9	26
15:4–5	92
15:16	72
17:2	72
17:3	118
17:6	72

Acts

2:23	127
3:15	127
3:21	120, 145
7:58	57
8:1	57
9:1–2	57
9:13–14	57
16:31	61
19:4	86
22:4–5	57
26:9–11	57

Romans

1—3	47, 68
1	14
2	14
5	50
1:21—3:18	107
1:30–31	130
1:18	14, 24, 79, 108
1:21	15, 79
1:22	84
1:23	16, 108
1:24	79, 80, 103, 108, 135
1:25	15, 16
1:26	79, 80, 103, 108, 135
1:28	79, 80, 103, 108, 135
2:14–15	80
3:9	41, 70, 71
3:10	18, 49, 70
3:12	72
3:19–21	71
3:19–20	80
3:19	19, 47, 49
3:20	47
3:21–24	68
3:21–22	49, 68, 82
3:21	49, 80
3:22–24	50
3:22–23	17, 76
3:22	54, 56, 68
3:23	45, 47
3:24	47
3:25	21, 22, 50, 96, 97, 108
3:27	72
3:28–29	76
3:28	68, 69
4:2–3	46
4:2	70
4:3	51, 70, 90
4:4	70
4:5	70, 96
4:6	51, 70
4:11	71
4:13	47, 51, 71
4:17	75, 90, 91
4:18	88
4:19	51, 88
4:20	90
4:24	87
4:25	50, 52, 54, 144

Index

5:1	54	8:22	48, 82, 140, 145
5:2	54	8:23	82
5:6–11	56	8:26	116
5:6	18, 58, 58, 100	8:31–39	109
5:7–8	27	8:32	55
5:8	18, 58, 100	8:33	69
5:9	69, 72	8:35	107, 108
5:10	18, 55, 58, 60, 72, 96, 100, 116	8:37–39	48
		8:37	108
5:11	55	8:38–39	32, 107
5:12–21	37, 44	8:39	55
5:12	38, 39, 48, 70	9:8	119
5:14	38, 39, 79	9:25	31
5:15	38, 41, 45	9:33	31
5:16	38, 39, 40, 41	10:9	86
5:17–18	144	11:11	108, 124
5:17	39, 40, 41, 46	11:15	108, 114
5:18	39, 40, 41, 46, 48, 50, 52, 56, 57, 59, 60, 82, 96, 108, 132, 143, 144, 145	11:25	48
		11:26	48, 108, 109, 114, 139
		11:32	48, 78, 82, 95, 96, 100, 106, 107, 108, 121, 127, 132, 139, 146
5:19	39, 40, 42, 45		
5:20	48, 84		
5:21	18, 38, 39, 42, 55, 79	11:36	48
		14:7	139
6:3	55	14:8	139
6:4	55	14:9	139
6:11	55	14:10–11	6, 34, 61, 96, 121, 123, 139
6:16	18		
6:17	18	14:11	13
7:4	55, 80	16:26	99
7:5	80	16:27	55
7:6	80		
7:8	80	## 1 Corinthians	
7:11	80	1:18–25	27
7:12	80	1:25	33, 97
7:13	80	13:9	123
7:14	18	15:17	112
7:15	18	15:22	121, 139, 144, 146
7:24–25	55	15:23	112
7:24	81	15:25	146
8:1	55	15:51–53	83
8:17	55	15:53	121, 122
8:19–22	144	15:55	142, 143
8:20–22	99		
8:21–22	100		
8:21	18, 75		

Index

2 Corinthians
1:20	121
5:19	31, 96, 132
5:20	86, 132
5:21	28, 50, 52

Galatians
1:13	57
2:19–20	71
2:21	80
5:11	11
5:17	81

Ephesians
1:9–10	12, 20, 96
1:10	31, 35, 43, 60, 106, 120, 143, 145
2:1	92
2:5	92
2:8	74
2:10	74
4:18	18

Philippians
2:7	30
2:9–11	61, 96
2:10–11	5, 13, 75, 146, 147
2:12–13	92

Colossians
1:17	55, 130
1:19–20	146
1:20	96, 145
1:26–27	11
2:10	55
2:15	64

1 Timothy
1:13	57
1:14	74
1:15	74
3:16	27
4:10	146

2 Timothy
3:16	99

Philemon
1:18	52

Hebrews
1:3	28
3:12	86
9:12	97
9:14	55
9:15	55
10:12	55, 97, 132
10:14	55
10:22	86
11:6	86
11:39–40	121
13:20	97

James
1:17	26

1 Peter
2:9	124

1 John
2:1–2	100
2:17	121
3:23	86
4:7–8	24
4:8	25

Revelation
21	121
5:6	34, 96, 121, 124, 135, 140
5:8–14	43
5:9	34
5:13	xi, 34, 96
6:12–17	131
15:4	145
20:7–15	7
20:7–10	123

Index

20:8	123, 127	21:3	122
20:9	127, 129	21:4	142, 143
20:11	129	21:5	83
20:15	123	22:17	86
21:1	7		

www.ingramcontent.com/pod-product-compliance
Lightning Source LLC
Chambersburg PA
CBHW050817160426
43192CB00010B/1792